William Cobbett

The bloody buoy thrown out as a warning to the political pilots of

America

A faithful relation of a multitude of acts of horrid barbarity

William Cobbett

The bloody buoy thrown out as a warning to the political pilots of America
A faithful relation of a multitude of acts of horrid barbarity

ISBN/EAN: 9783744739214

Printed in Europe, USA, Canada, Australia, Japan

Cover: Foto ©ninafisch / pixelio.de

More available books at **www.hansebooks.com**

THE
BLOODY BUOY,

THROWN OUT AS A

Warning to the Political Pilots of America;

OR A

FAITHFUL RELATION

OF A

MULTITUDE OF ACTS OF HORRID BARBARITY,

Such as the Eye never witneſſed, the Tongue never
expreſſed, or the Imagination conceived,
until the Commencement of

THE FRENCH REVOLUTION.

TO WHICH IS ADDED,

AN INSTRUCTIVE ESSAY,

Tracing theſe dreadful Effects to their real
Cauſes.

BY PETER PORCUPINE.

" You will plunge your Country into an Abyſs of eternal
" Deteſtation and Infamy, and the Annals of your boaſted Revo-
" lution will ſerve as a BLOODY BUOY, warning the Nations of
" the Earth to keep Aloof from the mighty Ruin."
Abbe Maury's Speech to the National Aſſemb'y.

PHILADELPHIA PRINTED.

LONDON REPRINTED, AND SOLD BY J. OWEN,
No. 168, PICCADILLY.

DEDICATION.

To all the juſt and humane people in the United States of America, of whatever ſect or nation, this work is moſt re- ſpectfully dedicated, by their

Obliged and

Humble Servant,

P. PORCUPINE.

T A B L E

Of some of the most striking Facts.

A 3

T A B L E. v

INTRODUCTION.

THE object of the following work is to give the people of this happy land a ftriking and experimental proof of the horrible effects of anarchy and infidelity.

The neceffity of fuch an undertaking, at this time, would have been, in a great meafure, precluded, had our public prints been conducted with that impartiality and undaunted adherence to truth, which the interefts of the community and of fuffering humanity demanded from them. But, fo far from this, the greateft part of thofe vehicles of information have moft induftrioufly concealed, or gloffed over, the actions as well as the motives of the ruling powers in France; they have extenuated all their unheard-of acts of tyranny, on the falfe but fpecious pretence, that they were conducive to the eftablifhment of a free government; and, one of the editors has not blufhed to declare, that " It would be *an eafy matter* " *to apologize for all the maffacres* that have " taken place in that country."

We have feen, indeed, fome exceptions; fome few prints that have not difhonoured themfelves by going this length : but even thefe have obferved a timid filence, and

have avoided fpeaking of the fhocking barbarities of the French, with as much caution
as if we were to partake in the difgrace,
and as if it was in our power to hide them
from the world and from pofterity. If they
have now and then given way to a juft indignation, this has been done in fuch a
manner, and has been fo timid, as to do
them but little honour. They have acted
the part of the tyrannized people of Paris :
they have huzza'd every fucceeding tyrant,
while on the theatre of power, and, the inftant he was transferred to a fcaffold, they
have covered him with reproach. They
have attributed to factions, to individuals,
what was the work of the national reprefentatives, and of the nation itfelf. They
have, in fhort, inveighed againft the murderers of the fallen affaffins, while they have,
in the fame breath, applauded the principles on which they acted, and on which
their furvivors and their partizans do ftill
act.

Thus has the liberty of the prefs, a liberty of which we fo juftly boaft, been not only
ufelefs to us during this terrible convul-
fion of the civilized world, but has been
fo perverted as to lead us into errors, which
had well nigh plunged us into the fituation
of our diftracted allies. Nor are we yet
fecure. Diforganizing and blafphemous

principles have been diſſeminated among us with but too much ſucceſs; and, unleſs we profit from the awful example before us, we may yet experience all the calamities that heaven and earth now call on us to deplore.

Fully impreſſed with this perſuaſion, the author of theſe ſheets has ventured to undeceive the miſguided; to tear aſide the veil, and ſhew to a yet happy people the dangers they have to fear. With this object in view, he has too much confidence in the good ſenſe and piety of the major part of his countrymen, not to be aſſured, that his efforts will be ſeconded by their zeal in the cauſe of order and religion.

The materials for the work have been collected from different publications, *all written by Frenchmen*, and all, except one, from which only a few extracts were made, *printed at Paris.*

Well aware that perſons of a certain deſcription will leave nothing untried to diſcredit a performance of this nature, the author has taken particular care to mention the work, and even the page, from which each fact is extracted.

He foreſees that the cant of *modern patriotiſm* will be poured forth againſt him on this occaſion. He knows that he ſhall be repreſented as an enemy of the French na-

tion and of the caufe of liberty.   To this he,
will anfwer before hand, with the franknefs
of a man who thinks no freedom equal to
that of fpeaking the truth.   As to the individuals compofing this formerly amiable nation, many of them, and he hopes very
many, are ftill intitled to his love and
efteem.   He has, from his infancy, been an
admirer of their fprightly wit ; he owes a
thoufand obligations to their officious hofpi-
tality, and has long boafted of their friendfhip.   But, with refpect to the *regenerated*
French, he would blufh to be thought their
friend, after what he has recorded in this
volume.—And, as to the caufe of liberty, if
that caufe is to be maintained by falfehood,
blafphemy, robbery, violation and murder,
he is, and trufts he ever fhall be, its avowed
and mortal enemy.

THE

BLOODY BUOY, &c.

CHAP. I.

Facts taken from *L'Hiſtoire du Clergé François,* or, *The Hiſtory of the French Clergy,*
by the Abbé *Barruel.*

IT will be recollected by the greateſt part
of my readers, that, ſoon after the beginning of the French Revolution, the National Aſſembly conceived the plan of deſtroying the religion of their forefathers.
In order to effect this they ſeparated the
Gallican church from that of Rome, and
impoſed an oath on the clergy, which they
could not take, without becoming apoſtates
in the fulleſt ſenſe of the word. All the
worthy and conſcientious part of that body

B

refufed of courfe, and this refufal was made
a pretext to drive them from their livings,
and fill the vacancies with fuch as had more
pliant confciences, principles better adapted
to the impious fyftem, which the leaders in
the Affembly had prepared for their too cre-
dulous countrymen.

The ejeftment of the priefthood was attended with numberlefs acts of moft atrocious and wanton cruelty : thefe have been
recorded by the *Abbé Barruel*, in a work entitled, *The Hiftory of the French Clergy*;
and, though what is here to be found will
dwindle into nothing, when compared to
.what I have extracted from other works,
yet it could not be wholly omitted, without
fhowing a degree of infenfibility for the fufferings of thefe men, that I am perfuaded the
reader would not have excufed. I fhall therefore begin the relation with fome extracts from
that work.

It will be obferved, that thefe extracts,
as well as all thofe that compofe this compi-
lation, are an abridged tranflation from the
French; but, as far as relates to thofe contained in this chapter, the American reader
may eafily verify the tranflation by exa-
mining the Englifh edition of the Abbé
Barruel's work, which is to be found in
moft parts of the Union.

Soon after the firſt National Aſſembly
had decreed, that the Comtat of Avignon
b ..ged to the French nation, an army of
a dins, of whom one Jourdan, ſur-named
t Cut-throat, was the commander, took
poſſeſſion of the unfortunate city of Avignon. The churches were immediately pillaged, the ſacred vaſes profaned and carried
off, and the altars levelled to the ground.
The priſons were ſoon filled, and the unhappy victims were releaſed only to ſuffer
death. A deep pit was dug to receive their
dead bodies, ſix hundred of which were
thrown into it, mangled and diſtorted, before ten o'clock the next day. Among
them was Mr. Nolhac, a prieſt, in the eigh-
tieth year of his age. He had been thirty
years rector of St. Symphorien, a pariſh
which he preferred to all others, and which
he could not be prevailed on to quit for a
more lucrative one, becauſe he would not
deſert the poor. During his rectorſhip he
had been the common father of his pariſhioners, the refuge of the indigent, the com-
forter of the afflicted, and the fiend and
counſellor of every honeſt man. When
the hour of danger approached, his friends
adviſed him to fly; but no intreaties could

prevail on him to abandon his flock: " No," said the good old man, " I have watched " over them in the halcyon days of peace, " and shall I now leave them midst storms " and tempests, without a guide; without " any one to comfort them in their last " dreary moments ?"—Mr. Nolhac, who, till now, had been respected even by the Cut-throats, was sent to the prison the evening before the execution. His appearance and his salutation, were those of a consoling an-gel: " I come, my children, to die with " you: we shall soon appear in the presence " of that God whom we serve, and who will " not desert us in the hour of death." He fortified their drooping courage, administered the last consolatory pledges of his love, and, the next day embraced and cheered each in-dividual as he was called forth by the mur-derers. Two of these stood at the door with a bar of iron in their hands, and as the pri-soners advanced knocked them down: the bodies were then delivered over to the other ruffians, who hacked and disfigured them with their sabres, before they threw them into the pit, that they might not after-wards be known by their friends and re-lations.—When the Cut-throats were dis-persed, every one was anxious to find the body of Mr. Nolhac. It was at last discovered by the cassock, and the crucifix which he wore on his breaſt. It had been pierced in fifty places, and the ſkull was maſhed to pieces.

Page 210.

Several prieſts were conducted to La-grave, where they were told that they muſt take the oath,* or ſuffer death. Among them was Sulpician of 98 years of age, and a young Abbé of the name of Novi. The whole choſe death, the venerable Sulpician leading the way. The trial of Mr. Novi was particularly ſevere. The ruffians brought his father to the ſpot, and told him, if he could perſuade his ſon to ſwear, he ſhould live. The tender old man, wavering, heſitating between the feelings of nature and the duties of religion, at laſt yields to pa-rental fondneſs, throws his arms round his child's neck, buries his face in his boſom, and with tears and ſobs preſſes his compli-ance. " Oh ! my child, my child, ſpare the " life cf your Father !"—" My deareſt Fa-

---

* This oath amounted to neither more nor leſs than direct perjury ſince, by taking it, they muſt break the oath they had made when they entered the prieſthood.

B 3

" ther!—My deareft Father," returned the
Abbe, " I will do more. I will do more.
" I will die worthy of you and my God.
" You educated me a Catholic: I am a
" prieft, a fervant of the Lord. It will
" be a greater comfort to you, in your
" gray hairs, to have your fon a martyr
" than an apoftate."—The villains tear them
afunder, and amidft the cries and lamentations of the father, extend the fon before him
a bleeding corps.

PAGE 211.

In the fame town, and on the fame day,
the axe was fufpended over the head of Mr.
Teron, when the revolutionifts bethought
them that he had a fon. This fon was a-
bout ten years of age, and, in order to enjoy the father's torments, and the child's
tears both at a time, he was brought to the
place of execution. His tears and cries gave
a relifh to the ferocious banquet. After tir-
ing themfelves with the fpectacle, they put
the father to death before the eyes of the
child, whom they befmeared with his blood.

After having fpoken of the conduct of the magiftrates and mob at Bourdeaux, the hiftorian mentions the death of Mr. Langoiran and the Abbé Dupuis, thus.

At the entrance of the court-houfe, the Abbé Dupuis received a firft wound; others foon levelled him to the ground. A young lad, of about fifteen or fixteen, cut a hole in the cheek with a knife, to hold up the head by, while others were employed in haggling it from the body, which was ftill in agonies. This operation not fucceeding in fuch a crowd, they took hold of the legs, and dragged the carcafe about the ftreets and round the ramparts.

Mr. Langoiran had but juft fet his foot on the firft ftep of the ftairs, when he was knocked down. His head was hacked off in an inftant, and a ruffian held it up, crying aloud: " off with your hats! long live the " nation." The bareheaded populace anfwered: " long live the nation." The head was then carried round the town in fignal of a triumph, gained by a tumultuous populace and ten thoufand foldiers under arms, over a poor defencelefs prieft.

The 14th of July, fo famous in the annals of the Revolution, was this year celebrated at Limoges, by the death of Mr. Chabrol. He was a moft ufeful member of fociety; diftinguifhed round his neighbourhood as a bone-fetter; he was at once the furgeon and the paftor of his parifhioners; and among his murderers were fome of thofe who owed to him the ufe of their limbs. He was of a quick and impetuous temper, and indued with uncommon bodily ftrength. His death certainly was not that of a chriftian martyr; but it deferves particular notice, as a ftriking proof of the cowardly ferocity of the French populace.

He had taken fhelter at a magiftrate's, and begged leave to elude the mob by going out of the houfe the back way; but the magiftrate durft not comply. He was forced to face his blood-thirfty purfuers. The indignant prieft met them at the door; the attack inftantly began. Without a fingle weapon of defence, he had to encounter hundreds of the mob, armed with clubs, guns, fabres, and knives; but, notwithftanding the amazing inequality, he held them a long time at bay. Some he felled to the ground, others ran from him; he tore a bayonet out of his flefh, and ftabbing it into the breaft of his adverfary, fent him to die among the crowd. At laft, weakened with the lofs of blood, he falls, and the bafe and mercilefs fcoundrels cry, *to the lamp-poft*. The idea of hanging reanimates the remaining drops in his veins. He rifes upon his legs for the laft time; but numbers prevailed; again he falls, covered with wounds, and expires. His laft groan is followed by the ferocious howl of *victory*; the daftardly affaffins fet no bounds to their infults; they cut and hacked his body to pieces, and wrangled for the property of his ragged and bloody caffock.

***

PAGE 268.

As foon as the unfortunate Louis XVI. had been transferred from his throne to a loathfome prifon, the National Affembly formed a plan for the total extirpation of the priefts, and with them the Chriftian Religion. The minifters of the altar were feized and thrown into prifon, or tranfported, from every part of the country. At Paris about three hundred of them were fhut up, in order to be maffacred, and were actually put to death during the firft and fecond weeks of September, 1792.

About one hundred and eighty of thefe unhappy men were confined in the convent of the Carmelites. A troop of affaffins commenced the maffacre in the garden, where the priefts were permitted to take the air; but while they were proceeding, a commiffary arrived, and informed them that the work was not to go on that way. There were now about a hundred left alive, who were all ordered into the fanctuary of the church; but, to get thither, they had to pafs through a crowd of their murderers. One received a ball, another a blow, and another a ftab : fo that, when arrived in the fanctuary, they prefented a fcene, the moft heart-piercing that eyes ever beheld. Some were dragged in wounded, others quite dead. Even here, though furrounded by a detachment of foldiers, the blood-thirfty mob rufhed in upon them, and murdered feveral at the very altar. The fanctuary of a Chriftian church was, for the firft time fince the bleffed Redeemer appeared among men, filled with a promifcuous group of the living, the dying, and the dead. The marble pavement was covered with dirt and gore and mangled carcafes, and the fides of the altar fplafhed with blood and brains.

The foldiers had not been brought to fave the lives of the priefts : the commiffary who headed them was to execute a plan of more deliberate murder. The furviving priefts were called out two at a time, and murdered in the prefence of the commiffary, who took their names down in a book, as he was anfwerable for their affaffination. Of all that were found here, only four or five efcaped — The like undiftinguifhed carnage was exhibited at the other prifons.

Every one of thefe men might have faved his life by taking the proffered oath, yet not one of them condefcended to do it. Let the infidel fhow us, if he can, any thing like this in the annals of his impious feft.

⟩⟩ ⟨⟨⟨⟩⟩ ⟨⟨⟩⟩ ⟨⟨⟩⟩ ⟨⟨⟩

PAGE 318.

At the gate of the prifon of La Force, the affaffins were placed in two rows : the two ruffians, called judges, who gave the fignal of death, were placed at the gate; and, as foon as the prifoner paffed them, the affaffins difpatched him with their knives or fabres, throwing the bodies in a heap at the end of the line. At the foot of this trophy of dead bodies, fays the hiftorian, we muft now exhibit a fcene of a different kind, in the murder of the princefs of Lamballie. She had retired in fafety to London ; but her attachment to the royal family would not fuffer her to remain in her afylum, while they were expofed. Her fidelity was a crime that the infidelity of her enemies could never forgive.

When this illuftrious victim was brought forth, fhe was afked to fwear an eternal hatred to the king, the queen, and to royalty. " The oath," faid fhe, " is foreign to " the fentiments of my heart, and I will " never take it."—She was inftantly delivered over to the minifters of death. Thefe ruffians pretend to carefs her, ftroke her cheeks with their hands yet reeking with human blood, and thus conduct her along the line. Amidft all thefe infults her courage never deferted her. When arrived at the heap of dead bodies, fhe was ordered to kneel, and afk pardon of the nation: " I have never injured the nation," fhe replied, " nor will I afk it's pardon."— " Down," faid they, " and afk pardon, if " you wifh to live." " No," faid fhe, " I " fcorn to afk pardon from affaffins that " call themfelves the nation: I will never " bend my knee, or accept of a favour at " fuch hands."

Her foul was fuperior to fear. " Kneel and " afk pardon," was heard from a thoufand voices, but in vain. Two of the affaffins now feized her arms, and, pulling her from fide to fide, nearly diflocated her fhoulders. " Go on, fcoundrels," faid the heroic prin-

cefs, " I will afk no pardon."—In a rage
to fee themfelves thus overcome by the conftancy of a woman, they dafhed her down,
and rufhed in upon her with their knives
and poignards. Her head foon appeared
hoifted upon a liberty pike, and her heart,
after *being bit* by one of the ruffians, was put
into a bafon. Both were carried in triumph
through the ftreets of Paris. At laft, after
having feafted the eyes of the multitude, the
bearers took them to the Temple, now become a prifon, where one of the two commiffaries that guarded the king, called him
to the window, that he might fee it; but his
companion, a little more humane, prevented
the unfortunate monarch from approaching.
A fainting fit, from hearing of the event,
fortunately faved the queen from the heart-
rending fight.

The body, ftripped naked and the bowels
hanging out, was expofed to view on the
top of the murdered victim, where it remained till the maffacre was over.

PAGE 327.

A great fire was made in the Place-Dau-
phine, at which many, both men and women, were reafted. The Countefs of Perig-

C

nan with her three daughters were dragged
thither. They were ftripped, rubbed over
with oil, and then put to the fire. The eldeft
of the daughters, who was fifteen, begged
them to put an end to the torments, and a
young fellow fhot her through the head.
The cannibals, who were fhouting and dan-
cing round the fire, enraged to fee themfelves thus deprived of the pleafure of hearing her cries, feized the too merciful murderer, and threw him into the flames.

When the Countefs was dead, they
brought fix priefts, and cutting off fome of
the roafted flefh, prefented them each a
piece to eat. They fhut their eyes, and
made no anfwer. The oldeft of the priefts
was then ftripped, and tied oppofite the fire.
The mob told the others, that perhaps they
might prefer the relifh of a prieft's flefh to
that of a Countefs; but they fuddenly
rufhed into the flames. The barbarians·
tore them out to prolong their torments;
not, however, before they were dead, and
beyond the reach even of Parifian cruelty.

PAGE 328.

On Monday, September 3, at ten o'clock
in the evening, a man, or rather a monfter,

named Philip, living in the street of the
Temple, came to the Jacobin Club, of
which he was a member; and, with a box
in his hand, mounted the tribune. Here he
made a long speech on patriotism, conclu-
ding by a declaration, that he looked upon
every one who preferred the ties of blood
and of nature to that of patriotic duty, as
an aristocrat worthy of death; and, to convince them of the purity and sincerity of
his own principles, he opened the box, and
held up, by the grey hair, the bloody and
shrivelled heads of his father and mother,
" which I have cut off," said the impious
wretch, " because they obstinately persisted
" in not hearing mass from a constitutional
" priest*." The speech of this parricide received the loudest applauses; and the two
heads were ordered to be buried beneath
the busts of Ankerstrom and Brutus, behind the president's chair †.

* That is one of the apostates.

† According to Monsieur Peltier, in his picture of
Paris, the number of persons murdered in the different
prisons of that city, from Sunday the 2d to Friday the
7th of September 1792, amounted to 1,005. To these,
he says, should be added the poor creatures who were
put to death in the hospital of Bicetre, and in the yards
of la Salpetriere; those who were drowned at the hospital of la Force; and all those who were dragged out of

The laſt faƈt related is of ſuch a horrid nature, that, though ſo well authenticated, it would almoſt ſtagger our belief, had we not proof of ſo many others, which equal, if not ſurpaſs it. I ſhall here extraƈt one from *La Conjuration de Maximilien Robeſpierre*, a work publiſhed at Paris in the year 1795.

The author, after ſpeaking of the unnatural ferocioufneſs which the revolution had produced in the hearts of the people, ſays (page 162) I will here give a proof, and a ſhocking one it is.—Garnier of Orleans had a ſon, who had been intended for the prieſthood, and had been initiated in the ſubdeaconſhip; conſequently he was attached to the Chriſtian faith. His father one day ſeized him by the throat, and led him to the revolutionary tribunal, where he was inſtantly condemned ; nor would the barbarous father quit his child till he ſaw his head ſevered from his body. After the execution was over, the tribunal, ever as capricious as bloody, feigned remorſe, and were proceeding to condemn the father ; but the National Convention, informed of the affair, annulled the proceſs, and publicly

the dungeons of the Conciergerie and the Chatelet, to be butchered on the Pont-au-Change, which may be computed, without exaggeration, at 8,000 individuals.

applauded the conduct of the unnatural father, as an imitator of the republican Brutus.

In the extracts from the history of the French clergy, the propofed limits of this work has obliged me to forego the pleafure of mentioning a great number of facts, which reflect infinite honour on that calumniated and unfortunate body of men, as well as on the Chriftian religion. The following trait, however, I cannot prevail on myfelf to omit.

+c⊃✝✝⊂✝✝⊃✝✝c⊃✝⊂✝⊃✝

PAGE 341.

At Rheims lived a man, who, from the number of his years, might be called the dean of Chriftendom; and, from the fame of his virtues, the prieft, by excellence. He had long been known by no other name than that of the holy prieft. This was Mr. Pacquot, rector of St. Jonn's. When the revolutionary affaffins broke into his oratory, they found him on his knees. A true and faithful difciple of Jefus Chrift, he yielded himfelf into the hands of his executioners without fo much as a murmur, and fuffered himfelf to be led before the fero-

cious magiftrate, as a lamb to the flaughter.
He croffed the ftreet finging the pfalms of
David, while the fanguinary ruffians that
conducted him, endeavoured to drown his
voice by their blafphemies. At the threfh-
old of the town-hall an attempt was made
to murder him, but the mayor interfered,
faying to the people, "What are you about?
" This old fellow is beneath notice. He is
" a fool: fanaticifm has turned his brain."
Thefe words roufed the venerable old man.
" No, Sir," fays he, " I am neither a fool
" nor a fanatic, nor fhall my life take re-
" fuge under fuch an ignominious fhelter.
" I wifh you to know, that I was never
" more in my fober fenfes. Thefe men
" have tendered me an oath, decreed by
" the National Affembly. I am well ac-
" quainted with the nature of this oath: I
" know that it is impious, and fubverfive of
" religion. They leave me the choice of
" the oath or death, and I choofe the lat-
" ter. I hope, Sir, I have convinced you
" that I am in my fenfes, and know per-
" fectly well what I am about."—The
nettled magiftrate immediately abandoned
him to the mob. " Which of you," faid
the old man, " is to have the patriotic ho-
" nour of being my murderer?"—" I am,"
fays a man who moved in a fphere that
ought to have diftinguifhed him from a

horde of ruffians. " Let me embrace you,
" then," fays Mr. Pacquot; which he actually did, and prayed to God to forgive him.
This done, the hard-hearted villain gave
him the firft blow, and his companions buried their bayonets in his emaciated breaft.

The reader's heart, I hope, will teach him
the love and veneration, that every Chriftian
ought to feel for the memory of this evan-
gelical old man.

If the death of all the murdered priefts
was not marked with fuch unequivocal
proofs of conftancy and fidelity as that of
Mr. Pacquot, it was, perhaps, becaufe a like
opportunity did not always prefent itfelf.
One thing we know; that, by taking an
oath contrary to their faith, they might not
only have efcaped the knives of their affaffins, but might have enjoyed an annual in-
come. Their refufing to do this is an in-
controvertible teftimony, that they were no
impoftors or hypocrites, but fincere believers
of the religion they taught, and that they
valued that religion more than life itfelf;
and, this is the beft anfwer that can poffibly
be given to all the fcandalous and atrocious
calumnies that their enemies and the enemies of Chriftianity have vomited forth
againft them.

CHAP. II.

Facts *taken from* La Relation des Cruautés, *commiſes dans les Lyonnois.*

THE next work that preſents itſelf, following the chronological order, is *La Relation des Cruautés, commiſes dans les Lyonnois,* or *The Relation of the Cruelties, committed in the Lyonneſe.*

✦✦✦✦✦✦✦✦✦

Page 37.

The grand ſcene of deſtruction and maſſacre was opened in the once-flouriſhing and opulent city of Lyons, by a public profanation of all thoſe things that had been looked upon as ſacred. The murderers in chief, choſen from among the members of the National Convention, were a play-actor and a man who, under the old government, had been a bum-bailiff. Their firſt ſtep was to brutify the minds of the populace; to extinguiſh the remaining ſparks of humanity and religion, by teaching them to ſet heaven and an hereafter at defiance; in order to prepare them for the maffacres, which they were commiffioned to execute.

A mock proceffion was formed, in imitation of thofe obferved by the Catholic church, It was headed by a troop of men bearing in their hands the chalices and other vafes which had been taken from the plundered churches. At the head of the proceffion there was an afs, dreffed in the veftments of the priefts that the revolutionary army had murdered in the neighbourhood of the city, with a mitre on his head. This beaft, a beaft of the fame kind on which our Redeemer rode, now bore a load of crucifixes, and other fymbols of the Chriftian religion; having the old and new teftament tied to his tail. When this proceffion came to the fpot which had been fixed on for the purpofe, the bible was burnt, and the afs given to drink out of the facramental cup, amidft the fhouts and rejoicing of the blafphemous affiftants.

Such a beginning plainly foretold what was to follow. An undiftinguifhed butchery of all the rich immediately commenced. Hundreds of perfons, women as well as men, were taken out of the city at a time, tied to trees, fhot to death, ftabbed, or elfe knocked on the head. In the city the guillotine never ceafed a moment; it was fhifted three times; holes were dug at each place to receive the blood, and yet it ran in the gutters.

It were impoffible to defcribe this fcene of carnage, or to give an account of each act of the, till now, unheard-of barbarity: two or three, however, demand a particular mention.

PAGE 39.

Madame Lauras, hearing that her huf- band was condemned, went, accompanied with her ten children, and threw herfelf on her knees before the ferocious Collot D'Herbois, one of the members of the Con- vention; but no mercy could be expected from a wretch whofe bufinefs it was to kill. She followed her beloved hufband to the place of execution, furrounded with her weeping offspring. On feeing him fall, her cries and the wildnefs of her looks but too plain- ly foretold her approaching end. She was feized with the pains of a premature child- birth, and was carried home to her houfe, where a commiffary foon after arrived, drove her from her bed and her houfe, from the door of which fhe fell dead into the ftreet.

Two women who had perfifted in afking the life of their hufbands, were tied, during fix hours, to the pofts of the guillotine. Their own hufbands were executed before their eyes, and their blood fprinkled over them.

Mifs Servan, a young lady of about eighteen, was put to death becaufe fhe would not difcover the retreat of her father.

Madam Cochet was condemned for having put the match to a cannon during the fiege, and for having affifted in her hufband's efcape. She was declared, by two furgeons, to be with child; but this was a reafon of little weight with men whom we fhall by-and-by fee murdering infants, and even ripping them from the womb. She was inftantly executed.

To thefe facts I fhall add the death of Maupetit. He was made prifoner during the fiege, buried alive up to his neck, and in this fituation had his head. mafhed to pieces with fmall cannon balls, which his enemies toffed at it with all the infulting grimaces of favages.

At Lyons the prierts met with the fame treatment as at other places, and honoured their deaths with the fame unfhaken fortitude. Twenty-feven were exceuted at one time, not one of whom had condefcended to accept of the fhameful conditions that were offered, nor even to folicit a pardon from the vile and blafphemous affaffins. During this murderous work the city of Lyons was ftruck with terror. The members of the convention ftuck up a proclamation, declaring all thofe, who fhould exprefs the leaft fymptom of pity, *fpelled perfons.* When the blood had in fome meafure ceafed to flow, and the affrighted inhabitants ventured out of their houfes, they were feen walking along the ftreets with their eyes fixed on the ground: men no longer ftopped, fhook hands, and gave each other good morrow. The fear of death was ftamped on every face: children durft not afk after their parents, nor parents afk after their children.

The villages round about fhared in the fate of the city. An apoftate prieft conducted a gang of ruffians, who carried fire and death before them among thofe good people, whofe only crime was giving fhelter to perfons efcaped from the maffacre. The charitable hoft and his affrighted gueft were butchered together beneath the hofpitable roof, while the wives and daughters were referved to fatisfy the brutal appetites of the murderers.

In vain fhould I attempt to give the reader an adequate idea of the crimes committed, by the order of the Convention, in this part of France. The author of *La Conjuration de Robefpierre* fays (page 159) that in the fpace of a few months, the number of perfons, who were murdered in the Lyonnefe and in the furrounding forefts, amounted to two hundred thoufand.

D

I shall conclude this chapter with a fact or two taken from *La Conjuration de Robespierre*.

❮❮•❯❯ ❮❮•❯❯ ❮❮•❯❯ ❮❮•❯❯

Page 210.

Though no torments could go beyond the merits of Robefpierre and his colleagues, yet, even in the execution of thefe monfters, the Parifians difcovered fuch traits of fero-cioufnefs as fully proved, that thefe grovel-ling tyrants had done no more than what they themfelves would have done, had they been in their places.

Robefpierre had been wounded in his head and face; his jaws were held together with bandages; and the executioner, before he placed his neck under the guillotine, fuddenly tore off the bandages, letting his under jaw fall, while the blood ftreamed down his breaft. The poor deferted wretch was kept fome time in this frightful ftate, while the air refounded with the acclamations of the barbarous populace.

❮❮•❯❯ ❮❮•❯❯ ❮❮•❯❯ ❮❮•❯❯

Page 209.

Henriot had no other cloaths on but a fhirt and a waiftcoat, covered with dirt and

blood. His hair was clotted, and his af-
faffinating hands were now ftained with his
own gore. He had been wounded all over,
one eye he kept fhut, while the other was
ftarted from its focket, and held only by
the fibres. This horrid fpeftacle, from
which the imagination turns with difguft
and affright, excited the joy, and even the
mirth of the Parifians. " Look at the
" fcoundrel," faid they, " juft as he was
" when he affifted in murdering the priefts."
The people called on the carts to ftop, and
a group *of wom.n* performed *a dance* round
that in which the capital offenders rode.—
When Henriot was ftepping from the cart
to the fcaffold, one of the under-execution-
ers, to divert the fpeftators, tore out the
eye that was already loofe.—What a hard-
hearted wretch muft he be who could per-
form an action like this? and to what a
degree of bafenefs and ferocity muft that
people be arrived, who could thus be
diverted ?

⋘⋯⟫⋘⋯⟫ ⋘⋯⟫ ⋘⋯⟫

PAGE 163.

We fhall not be furprized that this
thirft for human blood, and delight in
beholding the torments of the dying, were

D 2

become fo prevalent, when we know, that *mock executions* was become *a fport*. The women fufpended to the necks of their fucking infants, corals, made in the fhape of the guillotine; which the child, by the means of a fpring, played as perfectly as the bloody executioner himfelf.

❧❧❧❧❧❧❧❧

PAGE 161.

What could be expected from an education like this? What could be expected from children who were taught to ufe an inftrument of ignominious death as a plaything; who were taught to laugh at the fcreams of the dying, and who, in a manner, fucked in blood with their mothers' milk? When affaffinations became the fports of children, it was no wonder that the fentiments of nature were extinguifhed, and that perfidy and inhumanity took place of gratitude, filial piety, and all the tender affections.

What I am now going to relate, the mothers of future generations will hear with affright.—A child of ten years of age had been fcolded, perhaps whipped, by his mother. He ran to the revolutionary tribunal, and accufed her of being ftill attached to the Catholic religion. The accufation was admitted, the boy recompenfed, and the mother executed in a few hours afterwards.

Tell us, ye mothers, for you only can know, what this poor creature muft feel at feeing herfelf betrayed, and ready to be deprived of life, by the child fhe had borne in her womb, who but the other day hung at her breaft, and for whom alone, perhaps, fhe wifhed to live.

⁂⁂⁂⁂⁂⁂

PAGE 162.

In fhort, fays the author, men contracted fuch a tafte as excites horror even to believe it poffible. God forbid that I fhould enter into particulars on this fubject. The bowels of the reader would not permit him to proceed. Suffice it to fay, that we have feen the time, when man was becoming the *food* of man. *Thofe who practifed anatomy* during the reign of terror, know but too well what I could fay here, if compaffion for the feelings of my readers did not prevent me.

I cannot quit thefe facts without once more referring the reader to the work, from

which I have felected them. I wifh him
not to depend on my veracity, for the truth
of what he may find in a book written on,
the fcene. *La Conjuration de Robefpierre*
is to be had almoft any where :. I have feen
above a dozen copies of it in the hands of
different perfons. It was, as I have already
faid, publifhed at Paris, and, therefore, we
may reft affured, that the author has not
exaggerated ; but, on the contrary, we fee
by the laft article here quoted, that he was
afraid to fay all that truth would have war-
ranted.

·⫸⫷⫷·⫸⫷⫷⫸·⫸⫷⫷·

C H A P. III.

FACTS felected from the *Procés Criminel
des Membres du Comité Revolutionnaire de
Nantes, et du ci-devant Reprefentant du
Peuple Carrier* ; or, *Trial of the Members
of the Revolutionary Committee at Nantz,
and of the Reprefentative Carrier.*

THE work which we are now entering
on was publifhed at Paris during the
laft year ; but, as an introduction to the facts

extracted from it, it will be neceſſary to give the reader a concife fketch of the progrefs of the Revolution down to the epoch when the work was publifhed.

The States-General, confifting of the three orders, the Nobility, the Clergy, and the Tiers-Etats, or Commonalty, were affembled on the 4th of May, 1789. The deputies were all furnifhed with written inftructions, in which they were pofitively enjoined to make no innovations as to the form of government. Notwithftanding this, it is well known, they framed a conftitution by which the government was totally changed, the nobility abolifhed, and the church rent from that of Rome. Their conftitution, however, though eftablifhed at the expence of thouſands of lives, and though one of the moſt ridiculous fyftems of government that ever was invented, did not fail to meet with partizans; and we have heard it extolled in this country as the maſter-piece of human wifdom.

This firſt Affembly, which has been commonly called the Conftituent Affembly, ended its beneficent labours on the 30th of September, 1791, and was immediately fucceeded by another, which took the name of the Legiflative Affembly. Moſt men of fenfe forefaw that the fecond Affembly would improve upon the plan of deftruction marked

out by the firſt. The Clergy and many
men of family and fortune had been already
driven from their homes and poſſeſſions, it
remained for the Legiſlative Aſſembly to
finiſh the work by ſeizing on their property
and expoſing it to ſale : this they failed not
to do. Perſecution and maſſacre increaſed
daily ; but as the ſmall remains of power
left in the hands of the king was ſtill an obſtacle, or rather the monarchy itſelf was
an obſtacle, they were determined to
get rid of it. On the 10th of Auguſt,
1792, the king was dethroned (his fate is
well known) and the daggers of the aſſaſſins
were from that moment drawn, never more
to be ſheathed, but in the heart of ſome innocent victim. We have already ſeen ſome-
thing of the maſſacres which followed this
event at Paris and other places ; but even
theſe are trifles to what was to follow.

On the 21ſt of September, 1792, the
third Aſſembly, generally called the National
Conventional, opened their ſeſſions, and,
though every individual member had repeatedly taken an oath to maintain the authority of the king, they at once declared
France to be a republic.

After the murder of the king, this Convention declared war againſt a great part of
the powers of Europe ; and, in order to be
in a ſituation to make head againſt their

enemies, feized on all the precious metals in the country, or rather they enacted fuch laws as obliged the poor oppreffed people to bring it to their treafury, and receive in exchange a vile and worthlefs paper money. The churches were inftantly pillaged, and no perfon dared appear with a watch, or any other article in gold or filver.

The violation of property was only a part of their plan. The hearts of the lower orders of the people were to be hardened; they were to be rendered brutal; all fear of an hereafter was to be rooted from their fouls, before they could be fit inftruments in the hands of this hellifh Affembly. With this object in view, they declared our bleffed Lord and Redeemer to be an impoftor, forbade the acknowledgement of him, and the exercife of his worfhip. The churches were turned into prifons, ftables, &c. and over the gateways of the burial-grounds were written : " This is the place of " *etern..l fleep.*" Never furely was there a better plan for transforming a civilized people into a horde of cut-throats. It fucceeded compleatly. The blood now flowed at Paris in an unceafing ftream. A permanent tribunal was eftablifhed, whofe only bufinefs was to condemn, and certify to the Convention that the executions went on according to the lifts fent from its committees.

Befides legions of executioners there were others of affaffins. The command of thefe latter was given to thofe members of the Convention who were fent into the different parts of the country. Terror preceded thefe harbingers of death, and their footfteps were marked with blood. The fword, the fire, and the water, all became inftruments of deftruction.

During this murdering time, which has juftly affumed the name of the *reign of terror*, the leaders of feveral factions of the revolutionifts themfelves received their reward on a fcaffold, and, among others, Robefpierre and his accomplices. When thefe men fell, the Convention, according to its ufual cuftom, afcribed all the cruelties, committed during fome time before their death, to them alone, and the people, always eager for blood, now demanded the heads of thofe whom they had affifted in the murder of their countrymen. By facrificing thefe its inftruments, the Convention faw a fair opportunity for removing the infamy from itfelf, and of perpetuating its power. In confequence, many of them were tried and executed, and among others Carrier (a member of the Convention) who had been ftationed at Nantz, with the members of the revolutionary committee of that unfortunate town. From the trial of thefe

men it is that I have felected the facts which
are to compofe this chapter. The trial was
before the tribunal at Paris, to which place
the accufed were carried from Nantz.

It has been repeatedly afferted, by thofe
who feem to have more attachment to the
caufe of the French than to that of truth,
that the barbarities committed in that country, have been by the hands of foreigners.
Such a ftory is impoffible, and even ridiculous ; but, however, it has induced me
to infert here a lift of the barbarous wretches
who were fo long the fcourge of the city of
Nantz, from which it will appear, that they
were all Frenchmen born and bred. This
is an act of Juftice due to other nations.

Members of the Convention on miffion at Nantz.

Carrier, *born in Gafcogny.*

*Members of the Revolutionary Committee at
Nantz.*

Goulin
Chaux
Grand-Maifon
Bachelier
Perrochaux   } *born at Nantz.*
Mainguet
Naud
Gallen
Duraffier

Leveque, *born at Mayenne.*
Bolognic, *born at Paris.*
Battalié, *born at Charité-fur Loire.*
Joly, *born at Angerville-la-Martel.*
Pinard, *born at Chriftople-Dubois.*

Carrier was the great mover, the affaffin-general; the committee were his agents, Some of them were always affembled in their hall, to give directions to the under-murderers, while the others took repofe, or were difpatched on important expeditions, fuch as the fhooting or drowning of hundreds at a time. They ftood in need, however, of fubaltern cut-throats, more determined and bloody than the people in general; and therefore they raifed a company, who took the title of the company of Marat, compofed of the vileft wretches that were to be found. Thefe being affembled together took the following oath before their employers.

➤➤➤➤➤➤➤➤➤➤➤➤

Vol. IV. Page 203.

I fwear, to purfue unto death, all *royalifts, fanatics* (Chriftians*) *gentlemen* (the French

---

* *Fanatic* is the name now given to all who remain attached to the Chriftian Religion.

word is *mufcadim*, which means a *gentleman*, or *well-dreffed man*) and *moderates* (moderate people) under whatever colour, mafk, or form, they may appear.

I fwear, to fpare neither *parents* nor *relations* ; to facrifice my perfonal interefts, and even friendfhip itfelf; and to acknowledge for parents, brothers and friends, nobody but the patriots, the ardent defenders of the republic.

*)>‹‹‹•›)> ›‹‹••)>‹‹‹•›)> ‹‹(•

Pity with me, reader, the poor unhappy people that were to become the prey of a fet of blood-hounds like thefe. Pity the aged parents and the helplefs babes, that were to bleed beneath their mercilefs fabres. If you are not endowed with uncommon fortitude, I could almoft advife you to advance no further : fifty times has the pen dropped from my trembling hand : Oh! how I pity the hiftorian that is to hand thefe bloody deeds down to our fhuddering and indignant pofterity !

E

Vol. I. Page 66.

Tronjolly, a witnefs, informs the tribunal, that the Company of Marat was at firft compofed of fixty perfons; that Goullin openly propofed that none but the moft infamous villains fhould be admitted into it; and, at each nomination, cried out, " Is there no " greater fcoundrel to be found ?"

On the 2 th of October, fays the witnefs, I heard Goullin and his colleagues fay, that they were going to give a great example; that the prifoners fhould be all fhot. I atteft that this fcene was ftill more horrible than that of the 22d and 23d of September. The Company of Marat were carouling round a table, and at the fame time it was deliberated whether the prifoners fhould not be maffacred by hundreds. In this deliberation, Goullin was for indifcriminate death : and thus were the prifoners, without ever being interrogated, or heard, condemned to die. There exifted no proofs of guilt againft thefe unfortunate prifoners; they were what were called *fufpected perfons*; the felons, and all *real* criminals were fet at liberty.

'' Carrier, in quality of member of the Convention, had placed a vile wretch at Pain-bœuf, named Foucault, to whom he gave an abfolute power of life and death.

Old men, women with child, and children, were drowned. no diftinction. They were put on board of lighters, which were railed round to keep the prifoners from jumping overboard if they fhould happen to difengage themfelves. There were plugs made in the bottom, or fides, which being pulled out, the lighter funk, and all in it were drowned. Thefe expeditions were firft carried on by night, but the fun foon beheld the murderous work. At firft the prifoners were drowned in their cloaths; this, however, appeared too merciful; to expofe the two fexes naked before each other was a pleafure that the ruffians could not forego.

I muft now, fays the witnefs, fpeak of a new fort of cruelty. The young men and women were picked out from among the mafs of fufferers, ftripped naked, and tied together, face to face. After being kept in this fituation about an hour, they were put into an open lighter; and, after receiving feveral blows on the fkull with the but of a mufket, thrown into the water. Thefe were called *republican marriages*.

On the 26th of October, Carrier, the member of the Convention, ordered me (the witnefs was a judge of fome fort) to guillotine indifcriminately all the Vendeans who came to give themfelves up. I refufed; but the reprefentative of the people promifed that his prey fhould not efcape him thus. In fhort, on the 29th, he had guillotined twenty-feven Vendeans, among whom were children of thirteen, fourteen, and fifteen years of age, and feven young women, the oldeft of which was not above twenty-nine. On the fame day twenty other perfons were executed without trial.

Carrier, the bloodieft of the bloody, harangued his agents fword in hand; he ordered a woman to be fhot at her window, merely becaufe fhe looked at him; he chofe, from among the female prifoners, thofe whom he thought worthy of his foul embraces; and, after being fatiated with their charms, fent them to the guillotine.

Obferve well, reader, that this was a *member of the National Convention*, a *reprefentative of the people*, a *law-giver*.

⋙⋘⋙⋘⋙⋘⋙⋘

Vol. IV. Page 155.

I think it neceffary to bring in here a depofition or two from the third and fourth volumes of the trial, as they will fhow at once the pretended and real motives of the member of the convention and his committee.

Jomard, a witnefs, declares that, when the general was beat at Nantz, and the feizure of *fufpeted perfons* began, nobody belived any thing of a confpiration againft the republic. As a clear proof of this, adds *Jomard*, Richard, one of the agents of the revolutionary committee, wrote to his friend Crefpin, telling him that he had left the company of Marat without arms; but that means were found out to arm the patriots and difarm the *fufpeted*. The generale, adds Richard, is now beating; but do not frighten yourfelf; I will tell you the reafon *of this at your return*.

E 3

Latour, a witnefs, fays, I was fick ; Dul-
ny, who was my doctor, informed me that
Goudet, public accufer, had let him into an
important fecret ; which was, that Carrier
and the revolutionary committee not knowing how to fqueeze the rich, had fell upon
a plan to imprifon them, while they feized
on their effects. In order to have a pretext
for doing this, faid Goudet, we fhall give
out, that there exifts a confpiration againft
the republic. I am to make the general
beat early in the morning. The fans-culottes *, informed beforehand, are to pa-
rade at their different pofts ; the rich and
the timid will, according to cuftom, remain in their houfes ; to thefe houfes the
fans-culottes are to repair, pillage all they
have, and convey them to prifon.

Notwithftanding my illnefs, I had no in-
clination to be found at home ; I therefore
begged the doctor to give me notice when
the affair was to take place, which he promifed to do. In three days after he in-

---

* This degrading term, which is become the glory ·
of modern patriots, literally means, *men without
breeches*; but it was ever ufed by the French to defig-
nate vile, rafcally people, the dregs of fociety ; and as
fuch we ought now to underftand it.

formed me that the generale would beat the next morning. In f, ite of my ficknefs I went to my poft. We were all the day under arms, and a great number of rich people were pillaged and imprifoned, fome guillotined.

I atteft, adds the witnefs, that there was not the leaft appearance of any confpiration. All was a dead calm ; terror and confterna-tion alone reigned in the city. More than three thoufand victims to luft and avarice were this day lodged in loathfome dungeons, from whence they were never to be releafed but to be led to flaughter.

In fhall now infert an article or two that will give the reader an idea of the manner of proceeding of thefe fans-culottes.

❧✧❧✧❧✧❧✧❧✧❧

Vol. IV. Page 157.

One of the members of the revolutionary committee, with a company of armed ruf-fians, went to the houfe of one Careil. They firft examined all the papers, took 5000 livres in paper money, and 12 louis d'ors. They returned again in the even-ing, fays the witnefs, who it feems was miftrefs of the houfe ; we, at firft, took them for common thieves, and *therefore our alarm was not so great*; but, to our sorrow, we were soon convinced by the voice of Pinard, that they were the Patriots of the revolutionary committee. Our family was compofed of women and one old man. There was myfelf; four fifters-in-law, formerly nuns ; two old relations above eighty years of age, and my hufband. The houfe and yard were ftripped of every thing, and the ruffians were talking of fetting fire to the buildings. One of my fifters had made fhift to preferve 800 livres ; fhe offered them thefe to fave the houfe ; they accept the conditions, receive the money, and then burn the houfe to the ground.

Our perfons were now all that remained to be difpofed of. There was a one-horfe chair ; but which was too good for any of us ; it was faftened to the tail of a cart into which we were put (my hufband an old and infirm man being obliged to walk in the rear) and thus were dragged, preceded by our plundered property, to that gang of cut-throats called the revolutionary committee. Here our complaints were in a moment ftifled. Pinard faid, that his orders were to burn all and kill all. The committee were aftonifhed and offended at his clemency, and reprimanded him feverely for not having murdered us according to his orders.

. I, my fifters, and our poor old relations, were fend to one prifon, and my hufband to another. My hufband died, and we are only left alive to weep and ftarve.

It is well worth the reader's while to hear what this Pinard faid in his defence, on this head.

Vol. IV. Page 162.

We acted, fays he, by the order of the Reprefentative of the People, Carrier. When I went, at my return, to carry him the church-plate that I had taken from the nuns, he would infift upon my drinking out of the chalice (or facramental cup) and afked me why I had not killed all the damned bitches.

I fhall here obferve, once for all, that thefe volumes contain a feries of robberies of this fort. Sometimes the plunder was divided among the plunderers, fometimes it was delivered to Carrier, and at others it was depofited with the revolutionary committee. Thefe latter impofed immenfe taxes, or rather contributions, on the peo-

ple, under pretence of affifting the fans-
culottes, but which were applied to their
own ufes. It is juft to obferve alfo, that
the tribunal at Paris, before which they
were brought to anfwer for their crimes,
appears to have fhewn much more anxiety
about the gold and filver, than about the
lives of the murdered perfons.

VOL. V. PAGE 15.

Mariette, a witnefs, informs the tribunal
that he was detached on a party to feven
miles diftant from Nantz. The party,
fays the witnefs, went into the neighbour-
hod of the foreft of Rincé, and took up
their quarters in a houfe occupied by Mrs.
Chauvette. Five days after our arrival,
came Pinard, about midnight, and told us
that we were in the houfe of an ariftocrat.
He bragged of having that evening killed
fix women, and faid that Chauvette fhould
make the feventh. He threatened her, and,
to add to her torment, told her to comfort
herfelf, for that her child fhould die firft. It
is Pinard, adds he, that now fpeaks to you;
Pinard, that carries on the war againft the
female fex. I drew my fword, continues
the witnefs, and told Pinard that he fhould

ɔafs over my dead body to come at the
woman.

Commerais, who was another of this party, informs the tribunal, that Pinard being
thus ftopped, Aubinet, one of his companions, faid, ftand afide while I cut open the
guts of that bitch. He did not fucceed,
however, adds this witnefs. Now Marieuil
came up, and fwore he would have her life;
but finding us in his way, he faid, you
look like a good b—ger enough, I have a
word to fay in your ear.—We only want,
fays he, to know where fhe has hidden
ɔo,ooo livres belonging to a gentleman in
the neighbourhood. I anfwered, give me
your word not to hurt the woman nor her
child, and I will bring her forth. He promifed, and I brought them out. The woman, feeing that fhe was conducted to a
fort of cellar, cried out, I know I am
brought here to be murdered, like the women whofe throats were cut in this place
yefterday. All the favour I afk, faid fhe, is
that you will kill me before you kill my
child. She was now queftioned about the
money; but fhe continued her proteftations
of knowing nothing of it. Pinard and Aubinet prepared again to affaffinate her; but
they did not fucceed for this time.

The fame witnefs relates another adventure. When we were going hence, fays he, towards the foreft of Rincé, we heard a man in a little wood, crying for help. We found Pinard, and two other horfemen, each having a piece of linen under his arm. We left them, and foon after faw two poor peafants running away. In going along among the brufhwood, fays the witnefs, I heard fomething ruftle almoft under my feet: I knocked the bufhes afide with my mufket; what fhould it be but two children. I gave one of them, who was feven years old, into the care of Cedré, and kept the other, of five years old, myfelf. They both cried bitterly. Their cries brought to us two women, their mothers, who were alfo hid among the bufhes; they threw themfelves upon their knees, and befought us not to kill their children. In quitting the wood Pinard came up with us, he had feveral women, whom I faw him chop down, and murder with his fabre. What, fays he to me, are you going to do with thofe two children? ftand away, fays he, till I blow out their brains. I oppofed him, and while we were in difpute, two volunteers brought an old man, ftone-blind. This we now found was the grandfather of the children. Pray, faid the poor old man, take my life, and preferve my little darlings. I told him that we would take care of them; he wept and fqueezed my hand. This unfortunate old man, adds 'the witnefs, was murdered as well as the women.

Pinard quitted the high road in returning, for no other purpofe but that of murdering. He and his companions killed all they came at, men, women and children of all ages. To juftify his barbarity, he produced the decree that ordered him to fpare neither fex nor age.

❖❖❖❖❖❖❖❖❖❖❖❖❖❖

* My reader will recollect, that the National Convention of France had abolifhed *negro-flavery*; and he will alfo recollect, that the *humanity* of this meafure has been much applauded by thofe who have not penetration enough to fee their motive in fo doing.

We fhall now fee what advantage this liberty procured to the unfortunate country-people round Nantz. This city, from it's commercial relations with the Weft-India iflands, always contained a number of blacks who came to wait on their mafters, &c. As foon as the decree abolifhing negro-flavery appeared, thefe people claimed their rights as citizens; and, having no employment, they were taken into the fervice of the republic, and placed under the orders of the revolutionary committee. A party of thefe citizens were fent to affift in the murders round the city, and we fhall fee that they were by no means wanting in obedience to their employers.

✦⳽✦⳽✦⳽✦⳽✦⳽✦

VOL. V. PAGE 90.

An officer, named Ormes, came, fays a witnefs, to afk our affiftance in favour of five pretty women, whom the company of *Americans*, (this was the word which had taken place of that of *negroes*, becaufe the Convention had forbidden any one to call them *negroes*) had referved for a purpofe eafily to be gueffed at. A party marched off, and foon came to the houfe where the blacks had lodged the women. The poor creatures were crying and groaning; their fhrieks were to be heard at half a mile. The party ordered the door to be opened, which was at laft done. They then demanded the women; no, replied the blacks, they are now *our flaves*; we have earned them dear enough, and you fhall tear them away limb by limb if you have them. We are told thefe men, that, *thanks to the falutary decrees of the Con-*

vention, the French empire contained *no slaves*. The brutality of the blacks would not permit them to listen to the voice of reason; they prepared for the *defence of their prey*, when the party, always guided by *prudence, preferred retiring, to avoid slaughter*.

Two days after, continues the witness, the *Americans*, satiated with their captives, left them. One of these women, the hand‑somest in the eyes of the blacks, had been obliged to endure the approaches of more than a hundred of them. She was fallen into a kind of stupor, and was unable to walk or to stand. The whole five were shot soon after.

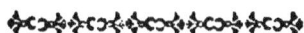

I do not know which is most entitled to our detestation here, the brutal negroes, or the pusillanimous, rascally Frenchmen, who were the witnesses of their horrid deeds. *Prudence* taught these poltroons to retire, when they saw five of their lovely country-women exposed to the nauseous embraces of a set of filthy merciless monsters! They saw them bathed in tears, heard their sup-plicating cries, were shocked at a sight the very idea of which rouses all the feelings of manhood; but *prudence* taught them to retire!—Savage villains! *prudence* never taught you to retire from the drownings and

F 2

fhootings of poor defencelefs innocent priefts, and women and children ! It was not till the blacks prepared to *defend their prey*, that *prudence* taught you to retire !

✦❀✧✦❀✧✦❀✧✦❀✧✦❀✧✦

Some of the women, taken in the country, were fuffered to die, or rather to be murdered, in a lefs fhocking way.

✦❀✧✦❀✧✦❀✧✦❀✧✦❀✧✦

Vol. V. Page 35.

Nantz, 5 *Ventofe, fecond year of the French Republic.*

Citizen *Malé* is hereby ordered to conduct the forty women, under his *care*, to the top of the cliff Pierre Moine, and there throw them head foremoft into the fea.

(Signed) Foucault.

We now come to the depofition of *George Thomas*, a health officer, who is one among the few, even of the witneffes, that appears to have preferved fome remains of humanity. He tells fuch a tale of woe as I hope, and am perfuaded, the reader's heart will with difficulty fupport.

The revolutionary hofpital, fays the witnefs, was totally unprovided with every neceffary. The jail-fever made terrible ra-
vages in all the houfes of detention ; feventy-
five perfons, or thereabout, died daily in
this hofpital. There were nothing but rot-
ten mattraffes, on each of which more than
fifty prifoners had breathed their laft.

I went to Chaux, one of the committee,
to afk for relief for the unhappy wretches
that remained here. We cannot do any
thing, faid Chaux ; but, if you will, you may
contribute to the caufe of *humanity* by a way
that I will point out to you. That rafcal
Phillippes has 200,000 livres in his clutches
which we cannot come at. Now, if you
will accufe him in form, and fupport your
accufation by witneffes that I will engage to
furnifh you with, I will grant you, out of
the fum, all that you want for the revolutionary hofpital. At the very mention of
humanity from Chaux I was aftounded : the
latter part of his propofal, however, brought
me back to my man. I rejected it with the
indignation that it merited.

I atteft, that the revolutionary committee
of Nantz feized and imprifoned almoft all

thofe who were efteemed rich, men of talents,
virtue and humanity.

I accufe this committee of having ordered,
to my knowledge, the fhooting or drowning
of between four and five hundred children,
the oldeft of which were not more than
fourteen years of age.

Minguet, one of the committee, had given
me an order to choofe two from among
the children, whom I intended to fave from
death and bring up. I chofe one of eleven
years old, and another fourteen. The
next day I went to the prifon, called the
Entrepot, with feveral of my friends, whom
I had prevailed on to afk for fome of thefe
children. When we came, we found the
poor little creatures ftood no longer in need
of our interpofition. They were all drowned. I atteft, that I faw in this prifon, but
the evening before, more than four hundred.

Having received an order from the mili-
tary commiffioners to go to the *Entrepot*, to
certify as to the pregnancy of a great number of women, I found, in the entering this
horrible flaughter-houfe, a great quantity
of dead bodies, thrown here and there. I
faw feveral infants, fome yet palpitating,
and others drowned in tubs of human ex-
crement. — I hurried along through this
fcene of horror. My afpect frightened the

women : they had been accuftomed to fee
none but their butchers. I encouraged
them ; fpoke to them the language of humanity. I found that thirty of them were
with child ; feveral of them feven or eight
months. Some few days after I went again
to fee thefe unhappy creatures, whofe fituation rendered them objects of compaffion
and tendernefs ; but—(adds the witnefs with
a faultering voice) fhall I tell you, they had
been moft inhumanly murdered.

The further I advanced, continues the
witnefs, the more was my heart appalled.
There were eight hundred women and as
many children confined in the *Entrepot* and
in the *Mariliere.* There were neither beds,
ftraw, nor neceffary veffeis. The prifoners
were in want of every thing. Doctor Rol-
lin and myfelf faw five children expire in
lefs than four minutes. They received no
kind of nourifhment.—We afked the women
in the neighbourhood, if they could not lend
them fome affiftance. What would you have
us do ? faid they, Grand-Maifon arrefls every
one that attempts to fuccour them.

prifoners, whom, for want of time to examine them, they had hewn down with fabres
under the window of their hall.

The witnefs adds, Carrier and the committee, as well as their under-murderers,
ufed to turn the drownings into jefts: they
called them *immerfions, national baptifms,
vertical tranfportations, bathings,* &c. I entered, fays he, one day a public houfe oppofite the Bouffay, where I faw a water-
man, named *Perdreau.* He afked me for a
pinch of fnuff: for, fays the ruffian, I
have richly earneft it; I have juft helped to
difpatch feven or eight hundred. How,
fays I, do you manage to make away with
them fo faft. Nothing fo eafy, replied he;
when I have a bathing match, I ftrip them
naked, two men with their bayonets pufh
them, tied two and two, into my boat,
whence they go foufe into the water, with a
broken fkull.

⟫⟫ ⟪⟪ ⟫⟫ ⟪⟪ ⟫⟫ ⟪⟪ ⟫⟫ ⟪⟪

Vol. II. Page 151.

Vaujois, a witnefs, fays; I wrote ten times
to the adminiftrators of the diftrict, and
went often to the revolutionary committee
to requeft, that fomething fhould be done
for the poor children in prifon; but could

obtain nothing. At laſt I ventured to ſpeak to Carrier, who replied, in a paſſion ; You are a counter-revolutioniſt : no pity : they are young vipers, that muſt be deſtroyed.— If I had acted of myſelf, ſays the witneſs, I ſhould have ſhared their fate.

One day, in entering the *Entrepot*, a citizen of Nantz ſaw a great heap of corpſes : thay were all of children ; many were ſtill palpitating and ſtruggling with death. The man looked at them for ſome time, ſaw a child move its arm, he ſeized it, ran home with it, and had the good luck to ſave it from death, and its more terrible miniſters.

Here *Thomas* is again queſtioned, and he atteſts, that the revolutionary committee iſſued an order, commanding all thoſe who had taken children from the priſons, to carry them back again; and this, adds the witneſs, for the pure pleaſure of having them murdered.

Coſſirant, a witneſs, depoſes that it was propoſed to ſhoot ſome of the priſoners *en*

maffe;* but that the propofal was rejected However, fays he, as I was returning home one evening, I met Ramor, who told me that the fhooting was at that moment going on. As I heard no noife I could not believe him; but I was not fuffered to remain long in doubt. A fellow came up to me covered with blood: that is the way we knock them off, my boy, fays he. Seven hundred had been fhot that afternoon.

❦❀❦❀❦❀❦❀❦

Vol. IV. Page 256.

Debourges, a witnefs, fays: I have feen during fix days, nothing but drownings, guillotinings and fhootings. Being once on guard, I commanded a detachment that conducted the fourth *maffe* of women to be fhot at Gigan. When I arrived, I found the dead bodies of feventy-five women already ftretched on the fpot. They were quite naked. I was informed that they were girls from fifteen to eighteen years of age. When they had the misfortune not to fall dead after the fhot, they were difpatched with fabres.

* The French expreffion is preferved here. It is to be hoped that it will never be adopted in the language of any other country. Its meaning is, *in multitudes.*

VOL. II. PAGE 244.

Naud, one of the accufed, fays; I faw red-headed general, named Hector, at the ad of a detachment conducting prifoners the meadow of the Mauves. Caftrie and followed him. When we came they were eparing to fire; but we made fhift to fave few of the children.

❧❧❧❧❧❧❧❧❧❧❧❧❧

VOL I. PAGE 27.

Labenette, a witnefs, informs the tribu- il, that the revolutionary committee or- :red to be ftuck on all the walls of the ty a decree, forbidding all fathers, mo- ers, hufbands, wives, children, relations, · friends, to *folicit* the pardon of any pri- ner whatever.

I was alfo witnefs of the drowning of nety priefts, two of whom, who were :crepid old men, by fome accident or other, caped, but were retaken and murdered. deed, adds this witnefs, I have been an re witnefs of feveral drownings of men, omen with child, girls, boys, infants, in- ifcriminately. I have alfo feen of all thefe :fcriptions fhot in the public fquare, and

at other places. The national guard of th
city was employed during fix weeks in filling
up the ditches, into which the maffacre
perfons were thrown. I was doctor to on
of the prifons, and was like to be difplaced
becaufe I was too humane.

VOL. I. PAGE 60.

Carrier fent for the prefident of the mi
litary commiffion. It is you then, fays he
Mr. fon of a bitch, that has dared to give
orders contrary to mine. Mind; if you
have not *emptied* the *Entrepot* in two hours
I will have your head, and the heads of al
the commiffion.—It is not neceffary to add
that he was obeyed.

VOL. I. PAGE 103.

Tronjelly, a witnefs, fays, that Chaux
expreffed his difapprobation of the law. o
the 14th of September. It is a great pity,
faid he, it ever was made; without that,
we would have reduced the inhabitants to
Nantz to a handful.—Carrier was confulted.
adds this witnefs, with refpect to receiving

money to save the lives of the rich; but the merciful reprefentative of the people anfwered — No compofitions; the guillotine; the guillotine; and take their money afterward. — Three women, too, charming certainly, fince they attracted the defires of the ferocious Carrier, had the   to be chofen for the tyger's pleafu firft facrificed them to his brutal lu then fent them to augment the *maffe* maffacre.

VOL. II. PAGE 175.

The widow *Dumey*, a witnefs, fays, that fhe is the widow of the late keeper of the *Entrepot*; that fhe faw fifty prieſts brought there, and robbed of all their money and effects; and that they were afterwards drowned, with fome women and little children. She adds, twenty-four men and four women were taken out one day. A child of fourteen years was tied with others to be drowned, his cries for his papa were enough to pierce the heart of a tyger; Lambertye tied him, however, and drowned him with the reft.

G

Fouquet, the companion of Lamberty, said on this occasion, that he had already helped to dispatch nine thousand, and that if they would but let him alone for twenty-four hours, he would sweep all the prisons of Nantz.

❦❦❦❦❦❦❦❦

VOL. II. PAGE 186.

Lacaille, keeper of another prison, called the *Bouffay*, gives a circumstantial account of one of the drownings.

The horrid night, says the witness, of the 23d of October, two soldiers of the company of Marat came to the *Bouffay*, each with a bundle of cords. About nine o'clock they told me there were one hundred and fifty-five prisoners, whom they were to transfer to Belle-Isle, to work at a fortress. About an hour after arrived thirty or forty more of these soldiers. An order from the committee was produced for the delivery of one hundred and fifty-five of my prisoners. I observed to them, that several of the prisoners on the list were now at liberty, or in the hospitals.

They now set down to table, and after having supped, and drank heartily, they brought out their cords, and diverted themfelves a while in tying each other, as they intended to tie the prifoners. I then conducted them to the rooms where the prifoners were lodged. They inftantly fall to work, tying the poor trembling wretches two and two.

Grand-Maifon now entered the court yard, and hollowed out to them to difpatch. Goullin came ftamping and fwearing, becaufe the number on the lift could not be compleated. There were fo many fick and dead that they could not well be made up. I fent you fifteen this evening, fays Goullin, what have you done with them? I told him they were up ftairs. Down with them, fays he. I obeyed, and they were tied, like the reft. Inftead of one hundred and fifty-five, Goullin at laft confented to take one hundred and twenty-nine; but this number not being complete, the equitable and tender-hearted Goullin orders the remainder to be taken from the prifoners indiftinctly; and when this was done he marches off at the head of the affaffins to conduct them to the river, where they were all drowned.

The widow *Mallet*, who had firft been robbed of her property, and then imprifoned, gives an account of the manner in which she and her companions in captivity were treated.

I complained, says this poor woman, to Perrocheaux of a violent sore throat. That is good, said he, the guillotine will cure you of that.

One day Jolly asked if I was not the widow Mallet, and giving me a look, that makes me tremble even now, aye, says he, she shall drink out of the great cup.

In the house where we were confined, there was a great number of beautiful pictures. Some men were sent one day by the committee to tear them to pieces, which they did, leaving only one which represented *death*, and jeering with savage irony, contemplate that image, said they, to cheer your hearts.

We were in want of every necessary. Seven hundred of us were confined in this house, which, even as a prison, was too small for two hundred. Forty were crammed into one little chamber. During six or seven months we had no infirmary, or rather each apartment was one. The sick and dead were often extended on the floor among the living. How many have I seen struggling in the pangs of death by my side.

Grand Maison told me one day of an old quarrel: times are altered, says he, now I have you under my clutches.

Duraffier came one day drunk, and began to make out a lift for execution. His oaths and imprecations made us tremble; I was on the fatal lift, and I know not how I have escaped.

My old servant went to solicit for my removal, representing me as dangeroufly ill. Perrocheaux said to her, Let her die, you silly bitch, and then we shall have her house, and you will fare better with us than with her.

❈❈❈❈❈❈❈❈❈❈❈

VOL. II. PAGE 215.

Brejot, a witnefs, fays: there were fome women going to be fhot; one of them had a child of eleven months old at her breaft, which the affaffins would have fhot with it's mother, had not a foldier fnatched it from her arms. The babe was carried by a woman to Gourlay, a furgeon, who had the compaffion to take care of it.

VOL. II. PAGE 217.

Fournies, a witnefs, fays, that there were at one time, to his knowledge, ninety-fix priefts drowned in the Loire. Adds he, four of them got on board a Dutch floop lying in the river; but were retaken and drowned the next day. Foucault, in boafting of the fecond drowning of thefe priefts, fhowed, in a company where I was, a pair of fhoes he then wore, which he had taken from the feet of one of them.

❧❧❧ ❧❧❧❧❧ ❧❧❧❧❧ ❧❧❧❧❧ ❧❧❧❧

VOL. II. PAGE 220.

Jane Lallies, a young woman, confined on the general accufation of being an ariftocrat, informs the tribunal, that fhe was ma le cook in the prifon. One night, fays fhe, a number of the company of Marat came to the prifon. One Girardeau conducted the troop. Come, my lads, fays he, I muft go and fee my birds in the cage. Ducon, feeing fome of the prifoners weep, what the devil do you howl for, fays he, we want provifions here, and we are going to fend you off to get us fome, that is all.

Crefpin faid to me, in giving me feveral

blows with his naked fwoid: march, bitch, light us along: we are mafters now: your turn will foon come, when there is no better game.

Come, come, my little finging birds, faid Jolly; out of your nefts, and make up your packets, and above all do not forget your pocket-books; that is the main point; no cheating the nation. Ducon faid afide to Duraffier; are not they finely bit? Finding they did not prepare themfelves quick enough, he adds, come, come, time to drefs them, time to fhoot them, time to knock their brains out—I think that is plenty of time for them.

Duraffier kept bawling out, quick, b—gers, march. To a fick man, who walked with a ftick, he faid, you want no ftick; march like the reft, b—gers; you fhall foon have a ftick with a devil to you.

Ducon, as he went away, faid to the keeper, good-bye for this time; we fhall come again foon to eafe you of the reft: I think we have a pretty fmart haul for once.—Thefe poor fouls were all drowned.

VOL. II. PAGE 222.

Mrs. *Pichot*, living by the water-fide at Nantz, fays, that fhe faw the carpenters

bufy conftructing the lighters for drowning
the prifoners; and foon after, fays the witnefs, I faw, brought to be drowned at the
Crepufcule, a great number of women,
many of whom had fucking children in
their arms. They fcreamed and cried moft
piteoufly. Oh! faid they, muft we be put
to death without being heard!

Several poor women of the neighbourhood ran and took a child a piece, and fome
two from them. Upon this the poor creatures fhrieked and tore their hair worfe than
before.—Oh! my dear, my love, my darling babe! am I never to fee your dear face
again! Heavens protect my poor dear little
love!—Such heart-piercing cries were furely
never before heard! yet thefe could not foften the hell-hounds that conducted them.

Many of thefe women were far advanced
with child. All were taken into the boats,
a part were immediately difpatched, and the
reft put on board the Dutch floop, till the
next day.

When the next day arrived, fays the
witnefs, though we were all terror-ftruck,
many had the courage to afk for a child
apiece of thofe that were left alive; but the
hard-hearted villain, Fouquet, refufed, pre-
tending his orders were changed, and all that
remained on board the floop were drowned.

The same witness says, One day I saw several prisoners, brought from the *Entrepot*, deposited in a lighter with a neck. They were fastened under hatches, where they were left for forty-eight hours. When the hatches were opened, there were sixty of them stifled. Other prisoners that were now on board were obliged to take out the bodies. Robin stood on the deck with his drawn sword in his hand, and superintended the work. This done, all the prisoners on board were stripped naked, men, women and children of all ages from fourscore to five; their hands were tied behind them, and they were thrown into the river.

✦✧✦✧✦✧✦✧✦✧✦

Here the judge, if we ought to call a sans-culotte ruffian a judge, asked the witness if this drowning was performed by day or by night. By open day answers the witness. She adds, I observed that the drowners became very familiar with the prettiest of the women; and some few of them were saved, if it can be called saving, to endure the more than infernal embraces of these monsters.

Delamarre informs the tribunal, that there was a heap formed of the bodies of the women who had been fhot, and that the foldiers, laughing, called this horrible fpectacle the *mountain*, alluding to the mountain of the National Convention.

⬥⬥⬥⬥⬥⬥⬥⬥⬥⬥⬥⬥⬥⬥

Vol. II. Page 231.

Foucault having faid one day to Bachelier, that he had two cargoes to difpatch that night, Bachelier flings his arms round his neck, faying, you are a brave fellow, the beft revolutionift I know among them all.

This fame Foucault fired at his father with a piftol; and was looked upon as the inventor of the plugged-lighters for drowning the prifoners.

Delaffal, who appears to have been an officer of police, tells the tribunal, that one day he had taken up a woman of bad fame, who lived with Lambertye, one of the chief drowners. He came to my houfe, fays the witnefs, in a rage, abufed my wife, and cafting a ferocious look at my children, poor

little b—gers, fays he, I pity you; to-mor-
row you will be fatherlefs.

VOL. II. PAGE 252.

Cordn, one of the company of Marat, informs the tribunal, that he had feven thoufand five hundred perfons fhot at the Gigan, and four thoufand he had affifted to
drown.

VOL. II. PAGE 254.

Sophy Bretonville, a witnefs, attefts, that
Perrochaux came feveral times to her father's, under pretence of fpeaking to her
mother about the releafe of her hufband;
but that his real bufinefs was to make inde-
cent offers to herfelf. In fhort, fays the
witnefs, he made me an offer to releafe my
father, if I would fatisfy his luftful defires;
but, as I refufed, very well, faid he at laft,
I fhall go and do his bufinefs for him in another way.

A houſe was wanted for ſome perpoſe by the committee. Chaux was told that there was one in the neighbourhood; but that it was occupied by the owner. A pretty ſtory, ſays he; in with the b—,ger into priſon, and he will be glad to purchaſe his life at the ex-pence of his houſe.

When the horrible ſituation of the priſon-ers was repreſented to the committee, Goul-lin and Chaux replied; ſo much the better; let them die, it will be ſo much clear gains to the nation.

Jane Lavigne informs the tribunal, that, one night, Carrier came with Phillippe to ſup at her houſe. They were talking, ſays the witneſs, of the meaſures to be purſued. You are a parcel of whining b—gers of judges, ſaid Carrier: you want proofs to guillotine a man; into the river with the b—gers, ſays the Repreſentative of the people, into the river with them; that is the ſhorteſt way.

Mary Herau informs the tribunal, that fhe got admittance one day into a prifon where there were a great many women confined, feveral hundreds. I faw one amongft them, adds the witnefs, that was taken in labour; fhe was, however, ftanding up. Such an object I never faw; fhe was crawling with vermin; her lips were blue; death had already feized her.—To bear the fmell, in this infected abode, I was obliged to have the fmelling-bottle continually at my nofe.

In confequence of the permiffion granted me to chofe a child out of this prifon, I went to a room where there where three hundred or thereabouts, all of whom appeared dying or dead. I ftopped at the door (for the ftink was fuch that I durft advance no further) and called the children to me. Some of the little innocents raifed their hands, and others their heads; but only fix were able to get to me. I took one of them, and was alfo allowed to take a poor woman, whofe fituation and piteous moans moved me to the foul. I gave them an afylum at my houfe till the iffuing of the inhuman decree, which obliged me to return them into the clutches of the tygers. When this decree came out,

H

I applied to the wife of Gallon, one of the committee, begging her to intercede with her hufband for the prefervation of the woman and child I had taken : I will do no fuch thing, faid fhe ; and, if you will be advifed by a friend, you will not trouble your head about them.—They were reimprifoned, and I never heard of them more.

VOL. III. PAGE 14.

Mrs. Laillet informs the tribunal, that fix young ladies, of the name of Lameterye, were fent to the Bouffay. Carrier, fays fhe, fent an order to put them inftantly to death. The keeper of the prifon commiffioned me to communicate to them the fatal tidings. I called them into a room apart, and told them that the reprefentative of the people had ordered their execution.

The youngeft of them gave me this ring, (here fhe fhowed the ring) they threw themfelves on their knees, and called on the name of Jefus Chrift. From this pofture the ruffians roufed to conduct them to the place of death. They were executed, without ever being tried. While they were difpatching, twenty-feven men awaited the fatal ftroke at the foot of the guillotine.

It is faid, to the *honour* of the executioner, that his remorfe for having executed thefe young ladies was fo great, that he died in a few days afterwards.

I atteft, adds this witnefs, that I have feen numbers of naked bodies of women, lying by the fide of the Loire, thrown up by the tide. I have feen heaps of human bodies gnawed, and partly devoured by the dogs and birds of prey; which latter were con- tinually hovering over the city, and particu- larly near the water fide. I have feen num- bers of carcaffes in the bottoms of the ligh- ters, partly covered with water.

•》》《《••》》《《••》》 《《••》》《《•

VOL. III. PAGE 23.

Rénaudot informs the tribunal, that he faw a number of men conducted to the meadow, called the Mauves, and fhot.— Some of them who were not killed by the fufils, fays the witnefs, were difpatched with the fabre. A cannoneer, named Jacob, came up to me, and faid that it was he who had finifhed thofe who efcaped the balls. Their necks, fays this butcher, were juft the thing to try my new fabre.

H 2

Vol. III. Page 24.

I accuse, says the same witness, the committee of the murder of three nuns, with my children's maid. They were conducted by Jolly to the committee to take the oath of apostacy. Shoot no more, drown no more, said the nuns, and we will even take this horrid oath. This amounted to a refusal, and the consequence is too well known.

Vol. III. Page 25.

Captain Leroux attests, that the murder of the ninety priests was a most wanton act of cruelty, contrary to the professions of the committee itself; for that they were *only* to be sent, it was said, into perpetual exile. He says he was ordered before the committee, and threatened with imprisonment for having permitted two of them to get on board his vessel.

Captain Boulet, one day, in weighing his anchor, saw four or five hundred dead bodies raised up by the cables; and adds, that there were one hundred and thirty women confined at Mirabeau, who difappeared all at once.

✠✠✠✠✠✠✠✠✠✠✠

VOL. III. PAGE 27.

Foucault, one of the accufed, being afked by the judge, what was become of the pillage of the priefts (for, as I have already obferved, this feemed to be the chief object of the trial), Foucault replied, that, having confulted Carrier on the fubject, he anfwered, b—ger! who fhould have it but thofe that did the work?—Foucault declares, that the effects of the priefts were lodged on board the covered lighter, whence the priefts had been precipitated into the water; and on board of which Lambertye, the chief in this expedition, gave a great dinner the next day, cofting forty thoufand livres. From other witneffes, it appears that Carrier affifted at this repaft, and that he even propofed dining on the fcaffold of the guillotine.

✠✠✠✠✠✠✠✠✠✠✠

The following traits are well calculated to fhow what fort of treatment a people muft ever expect from the hands of bafe-born

.villains, when they are fuffered to feize the
reigns of power.

✦❖❖✦❖❖✦❖❖✦❖❖✦❖✦

Vol. III. Page 11.

I had a fon and Daughter, fays a witnefs,
named *Pufterle*; Goullin had propofed a
marriage between his fon and my daughter,
and Goullin another between his daughter
and my fon. Neither had my confent; and
to avenge themfelves, when they were in
the committee, they feized my wife and
daughter, and all my moft valuable property.
The former were dragged to a loathfome
prifon; the latter I have never fince feen or
heard of.

✦❖❖✦❖❖✦❖❖✦❖❖✦❖✦

Vol. III. Page 17.

A friend of Goullin had, as he pretended,
been brought to punifhment by the family
of the two young Toinettes. When they
were brought before the committee, he told
them of this. But, faid they, it could not
be us. Goullin, like the wolf in the fable,
cried out, if it was not you, it was your
father. The two Toinettes were executed.

VOL. III. PAGE 33.

' My fon-in-law, fays a witnefs, named Vallé, had been confined for no other fpe-cified crime than that of being a *well-dreſſed man* (mufcadin). I went to Carrier and to the committee to folicit his releafe, before the order was iffued forbidding all foiicita-tions. There feemed to be fome hopes of fucceeding; but Chaux oppofed my requeft, and he alone. It was he who had ordered him to be imprifoned, to be revenged on us, becaufe we refufed to fell him a quan-tity of ftarch that he had a mind to.

VOL. III. PAGE 38.

I was at a drowning, fays *Tabouret*, on board a lighter conducted by Affilé. Come on, my lads, faid he, to the ifland of *Top-fy-turvy*. Before we got out to the finking place, I heard the prifoners make the moft terrible lamentations. Save us ! oh ! fave us ! cried they ; there is yet time ! oh ! pray, pray, fave us ! Some of their hands were untied, and they ran them through the railing, crying, mercy! mercy! It was then that I saw the villain, Grand-Maifon, chop off their hands and arms with his fabre. Ten minutes after, I heard the carpenters, placed in the little boats, hammering at the fides of the lighter; and, directly, down it went to the bottom.

⁂◆❂◆❂◆❂◆❂◆❂◆❂◆.

VOL. III. PAGE 90.

Trappe. When the fifty-five priefts were drowned, I went to Carrier to afk him what fhould be done with their money, gold and filver fnuff boxes, rings, &c. Leave them, nothing fays he. Embark thefe b—gers, and let me hear no more of them, fays the reprefentative of the people.

Thefe priefts, fays the witnefs, had a great number of valuable jewels, which were all delivered to Richard. Carrier, upon hearing that the expedition was over, feemed angry; blaft it, fays he, I intended to referve that job for Lambertye.

The widow *Dumey* corroborates the evidence of Trappe, and adds, after the priefts were drowned, Lambertye came to me, and pointing his fabre to my breaft, bitch, fays he, you fhall give me an account of the fpoils of thofe priefts.—I atteft, fays this witnefs, that Lambertye and Fouquet were the favourites of the reprefentative of the people.

Vol. III. Page 43.

Naudiller. I was, one day, at Carrier's, with Lambertye and feveral others. Carrier, in pointing to the river, faid, we have already ducked two thoufand eight hundred of them there. One of the ftrangers afking what he meant—Yes, fays Carrier, two thoufand eight hundred, in the *national bath*.

I myfelf faw, fays the witnefs, while I was at Nantz, which was not long, five hundred men and two hundred and fifty women, all tied, conducted to the Loire by Lambertye and Fouquet.

Vol. III. Page 50.

One time, fays *Affilé*, (he was one of the drowners) Fouquet ordered me to go to Marie, to befpeak the two lighters that were wanted for the night, and to engage fome carpenters. This done, I went and got the words, and the ſtaples to faſten the priſoners at the bottom of the lighter.—About nine o'clock nearly five hundred were put on board.—Theſe were pillaged and ſtripped in the lighter, and Fouquet ſwore, if I did not obey his requiſitions (which were always made in the name *of the law*) he would drown me with the reſt.

Four little boats, continues Affilé, attended each lighter. When the plugs were pulled out the priſoners cried, mercy !—There were ſome on the half deck with their hands tied only, and theſe, when the ſaw the lighter ſinking, cried, let us jump into their boats and drown them with ourſelves. But all that attempted it were hacked down with ſabres.

When the expedition was compleated, we went to Thomas's hotel, where the effects of the priſoners had been carried ; hence we went to Secher's, where we divided the ſpoil.

⟡⟡⟡⟡⟡⟡⟡⟡

The priſoners on their trial, having denied here, that they had given orders for the drownings, ſeveral of their orders were produced, and read. It may not be amiſs to inſert two or three of them. They will give the reader a perfect idea of the murderer's ſtile.

In the name of the Republic. The revo-utionary committee authorife citizen Af-ilé, jun. to require the number of carpenters hat he may find neceffary for the execution)f the expedition he is charged with. This :itizen is required to ufe all the difpatch in iis power, and to give *generous* wages to :he workmen, provided they work with all he *zeal* and activity that the *public fervice* :equires.

(*Signed*)   GOULLIN,
            BACHELIER,
               and others.

In the name of the Republic. The revolu-tionary committee anthorife citizen Golas to take as many lighters and fmall boats, as he fhall judge neceffary, for the execution of the *bufinefs* that the committee has en-trufted to his *zealous care.*

(*Signed*)   NAUD,
            BOLOGNIE,
            GOULLIN,
               and others.

In the name of the Republic. Citizen Af-filé, jun. is required to pay attention to, and fee executed, the order given to citizen Co-las; and all watermen and others are required to *aid* and *affift* in the *public fervice*, and to obey the requifition of citizen Affilé, under pain of being declared *bad citizens* and *fufpected perfons.*

(Signed)   GRAND-MAISON,
NAUD,
and others.

❧❀❧❀❧❀❧❀❧❀

VOL. III. PAGE 63.

Bourdin, a witnefs, gives an account of feveral fhootings. The laft that I faw, adds he, was of eighty women. They were firft fhot, then ftripped, and left expofed on the fpot during three days.

I carried a young lad off from the *Entre-pot*. He was thirteen years of age. When the revolutionary committee ordered all the children, thus preferved, to be given up, Jolly, who faid he was the judge of all the prifoners, permitted me to keep this boy; but my neighbour Aignes, who could not obtain a like favour, gave up a lad of fourteen years of age, agreeable to the order of the committee, and the next day we faw him fhot.

When the fhooting *en maffe* firft began the prifoners were fuffered to retain their clothes till they were dead. As they were conducted to the place of execution, and even after they arrived on the fpot, the old-clothes dealers were feen bargaining with the foldiers for their clothes. The poor unfor-tunate creatures had the mortification to fee their own towns men and women buying the poor remains of their fortunes on their backs; and, the inftant they fell, the mon-fters rufhed in, tearing the new-acquired property from their bodies, yet ftruggling in the pangs of death.—But, the revolu-tionary butchers found that this was but an unproductive fale: the clothes being fhot through funk their value; and this circum-ftance determined them to ftrip the prifoners naked before execution.

✦✦✦✦✦✦✦✦✦✦

Vol. III. Page 66.

Lambert, another witnefs, informs the tribunal, that he has feen the banks of the Loire covered with dead bodies; among which were feveral of old men, little chil-dren of both fexes, and an infinite number of women, all naked. One of the women, that I faw at one time, had an infant locked in her arms. She had been drowned at the

Crepufcule the day before with about two hundred more.

❦❦❦❦❦❦❦❦❦❦

Vol. III. Page 96.

A witnefs depofes that fhe faw Lebrun, one of the company of Marat, jump and dance upon the dead body of a child.

❦❦❦❦❦❦❦❦❦❦

Vol. III. Page 99.

Lamarie. I was one morning at break-faft with Crucy, Leveque, and Perrocheaux, when the latter told me, they were juft going to take a young girl out of prifon to put her in keeping for their own *ufe.*

I was one day, fays the witnefs, at the committee to afk the releafe of fome children, and I could not help being fhocked at the jocular manner in which they proceeded and talked. Chaux faid to me here we are, you fee, up to our eyes among the dead bodies and pretty girls.

❦❦❦❦❦❦❦❦❦❦

The criminals being afked what they had to fay concerning their having iffued certain cruel decrees, anfwered that they were *fathers of families*, and that if they had dif-obeyed Carrier, they feared he might not only deftroy them, but their wives and chil-dren alfo.

Now then, let us fee how thefe aff ctionate, tender-hearted fathers of families behaved towards the wives and children of others.

⦉⦊⦉⦊⦉⦊⦉⦊

Vol. III. Page 67.

As they had denied having iffued the cruel ord rs for imprifoning the children, the following decrees were produced.

The revolutionary committee orders the *be-nevolent* commiffaries of the 17th fection, as well as all others who have prifoners in their houfes of detention, to deliver to nobody, any child whatever; except it may be to the officers of the fhips of the Republic, and even they are to take *none under* feventeen years of age.

(Signed)   Goullin,
and others.

The citizen keeper of the *Entrepot* is or-dered to give in a lift of all thofe, who, in

I 2

obedience to the order of the committee, have delivered up the children they had taken from the prison.

(*Signed*)   CHAUX,
                                  and others.

Citizen Dumey is ordered to give in a list of all the persons, with the streets and numbers of the houses where they live, who have taken away any of the prisoners. He will be particular in the dwelling of the women, who, in spite of the decrees of the committee, has had the *infamy* to take away seven young girls of fifteen or sixteen years of age.

(*Signed*)   GRAND-MAISON,
                                  and others.

＊＊＊＊＊＊＊＊＊

When the blood-thirsty villains had thus collected all the unhappy prisoners together, they issued the following order.

In the name of the revolutionary committee of Nantz. The commandant of the troops is required to furnish three hundred regulars. One half of this detachment will march to the Bouffay, and, taking the prifoners thence, will conduct them bound, two and two, to the prifon of the Eperonniére. The other divifion will go to Saintes-Caires,. and conduct the prifoners from thence to the Eperonniére. Then, all thefe prifoners, together with thofe confined in the prifon of the Eperonniére, are to be taken and fhot, *without diftinction of age or fex*, in the manner that the commanding officer of the detachment may judge moft *convenient*.

(Signed) GRAND-MAISON,
GOULLIN,
MINGUET,
and others.

❅❅❅❅

In this place, it may not be amifs to let the reader hear what thefe monfters had to fay in their defence.

❅❅❅❅

VOL. III. PAGE 35.

Goullin. They keep telling us of our terrific meafures; I maintain that we made nobody tremble but the *mifers*, the *rich*, the *hoarders of provifions*, the *fanaticks*, and the

I 3

ariſtocrats; but as for the true ſans-culottes, they had nothing to fear.

Bachelier (VOL. III. Page 31.) *All the rich* were *ſuſpeǔted perſons.* We were obliged to ſtrike, not only them who *did,* but them who *could do* harm. However, very few patriots were ſacrificed; we aimed principally at the former nobility and clergy; at thoſe who hoarded up proviſions, and all ſuch as poſſeſſed great riches. The true and real ſans-culottes were ſpared.

❮❮«»❯❯❮❮«»❯❯ ❮«»❯❯❮«»❯❯

VOL. III. PAGE 99.

One day, ſays a witneſs, I begged Bachelier to have mercy on the little children. I pleaded their innocence, and repreſented their infancy, and the injuſtice of puniſhing them for the faults of their parents. Bachelier anſwered coolly, if I did not know you, I ſhould take you for an ariſtocrat. You do not perceive then, that theſe children have ſucked ariſtocratic milk; that the blood that runs in their veins is impure, and incapable of being changed into republican blood? I compare them, added he, to an oil-barrel, which, in ſpite of all the waſhing and ſcrubbing you can give it, will for ever retain its ſtink. It is juſt ſo with theſe children. They will always retain an attachment to the kings and priests of their fathers.

〓〓〓〓〓〓〓

Vol. III. Page 104.

Bachelier answers to this. With respect, says he, to the children of the aristocrats, I own that I said, they were hard to be made good republicans; and that it was much to be feared, that the children of fanaticks would *one day* refemble their parents. Renard, mayor of Nantz, who is known for a found patriot and a *humane man*, faid on this fubject, that the *cats* eat the *young rats*, and that they were in the right of it; for it was the only way of deſtroying the breed. I am perfuaded, adds Bachelier, that no true republican will blame me for faying and thinking like Renard, who was a moſt excellent patriot.

There was, it feems, another reafon for murdering the ariſtocrats; for when the propofal was made for killing them *en meſſe*, Robin faid (Vol. III. Page 85.) the patriots are *in want of bread*; it is juſt that thofe fcoundrels ſhould perifh, and not *eat up our victuals from us.*—Kermen oppofed this; but Robin exclaimed, none of your *moderate* propofitions here. I fay, they are a parcel of arift.crats that wifh to overturn the republic, therefore let them die.

Vol. III. Page 106.

Crefpin, one of the company of Marat, informs the tribunal, that he was at a drowning on board a lighter, where the prifoners were faftened down under boards, nailed from fide to fide. They uttered, fays he, the moft piteous cries. Some of them put their hands folded in a fupplicating pofture through the openings between the boards; and I faw the members of the committee chop off thofe hands and fingers. One of them plunged his fabre down in amongft the prifoners, and we heard a man cry out, oh! the rafcal! he has ftabbed me! —Our ears, adds the witnefs, were now ftunned with the cry of, oh! you rafcally, brutal favages! this is the mercy, this is the humanity of republicans!

One day, continues this witnefs, he faw Carrier in a coach at the foot of the guillotine, enjoying the fpectacle while about twenty perfons were beheaded.—Naud was with me, who went up to Carrier with me, and afked him, if he did not want a Marat.

Yes, b—ger, fays Carrier. I am your man then, faid Naud.

The new Marat was difpatched to call the *judges* to the reprefentative of the people'; and when Philippes ventured to tell him that, among thofe whom he had ordered to the guillotine from the Bouffay, there were two children of fourteen years of age, and two others of thirteen, Carrier fell into a violent paffion : damned b—gers, fays he, in what country am I got ? *All milk-hearted rafcals alike!*

⟶⟶⟶⟶⟶⟶⟶⟶

The following traits will prove that a ferocious cruelty had taken poffeffion of the hearts of the young as well as the old.

⟶⟶⟶⟶⟶⟶⟶⟶

Vol. III. Page 65.

Lalloue, fays *Naud*, offered himfelf as an exprefs to fetch back the one hundred and thirty-two perfons that were fent off to Paris. This, he faid, he would do for the pleafure of feeing them drowned.

This Lalloue, continues the witnefs, was a *judge*, and the companion of the reprefentative of the people, although but *nineteen* years of age.—He had been convicted of *theft*, and boasted of being one of the murderers of the prisoners at Paris, in the month of September, 1792.—Ah! says he, one day, to one of his companions on the bench, you should have seen us at Paris in the month of September. There you would have learned how to knock them off.

◄◄◄◄◄◄◄◄►►►►►►►►

Vol. III. Page 111.
Lecocq. I saw several men and women chopped down, on board a Dutch sloop that lay in the river. I saw a young lad assisting to drown the prisoners at the last drowning; particularly one whom he unmercifully seized by the leg, dragged to the side of the lighter, and kicked overboard.

◄◄◄◄◄◄◄◄►►►►►►►►

Vol. III. Page 126.
, *Laillet* informs the tribunal, that she saw a lad of about seventeen or eighteen years of age hew down two prisoners, and hack them with his sabre, at the prison of the Bouffay. They were afterwards, adds the witness, dragged to the waterside.

Fontbonne informs the tribunal, that, at the request of Delille, he went to the *Entrepôt* to endeavour to save an innocent and amiable family of females, the youngest of which was about thirteen years of age. Delille went with me. When we came to the prison, we were conducted to a horrid stinking hole under a stair-cafe. We asked for a candle, and, after some time, we got into this sort of dungeon. Here we found the mother and four daughters lying close to each other upon some wet and filthy straw; and round about them there were several dead women. The youngest daughter, whom alone we had obtained permission to take, was covered up in her mother's gown to keep her warm.—When we told the poor mother our errand; no, said she, my child shall stay and die with myself; we have lived, and we will die together.—We thought ourselves justified, adds the witness, in using force. When the mother perceived our resolution, she uttered such dreadful lamentations as are impossible to be described. My child! oh! my dear, darling child! were the last words her daughter ever heard from her. The child never recovered the ftroke; fhe pined away about eight months, and then died.

※※※※※※※

Vol. III. Page 113.

The fame witnefs fays, I faw a faw number of perfons conducted from the place of Equality, to be fhot at the Mauves. There were women and children of all ages amongft them. My heart could not fupport this fpectacle; I ran home, faddled my horfe, and rode to the place of execution.' When I arrived the poor creatures were all on their knees, and the foldiers were preparing to fire. I rufhed through them, and had the good fortune to fave eight of the children, the oldeft of which was twelve years of age; the reft were fhot with their fathers and mothers.

※※※※※※※

Vol. III. Page 114.

Laurency informs the tribunal, that he faw, at one time, three hundred men conducted to the water. They were all naked, and had their hands tied behind them. I faw too, adds the witnefs, feveral women and girls murdered, on board a barge in the river; two of whom, aged about eighteen years, I faw a young lad behead with his fabre, while he fung the *carmagnole*.

✤c⊃✤✦c⊃✤✦c⊃✦✤c⊃✦✤c⊃✦

Vol. III. Page 119.

Saudroc. At a great dinner, to which Lambertye, the chief murderer, invited Carrier, I was a witnefs of a moft fcanda-lous fcene. After the repaft was over, and while the glafs went round, Lambertye en-tertained us with a long and full account of a drowning he had performed the night be-fore, and boafted of the manner in which he fabred the poor wretches that attempted to efcape. All the *convives*, adds the wit-nefs, honoured his valour with long and re-peated burfts of applaufe.—Carrier toafted the *national bath*.—This monfter talked of nothing but death and the guillotine.

Another witnefs fays, (Vol. III. Page 123.) I faw Carrier, with his drawn fword in his hand, threatening to guillotine the firft perfon who fhould dare to fhow the leaft pity for the prifoners that were conducted to execution.

K

And another (Vol. II.) fays : Carrier came one day to look at the lighters that were conftructing for the drownings, and turning to Foucault, Charmingly commodious indeed ! fays he. Do you hear ? added he, pay thefe lads well for their labour.

❦c❧❦c❧❦c❧❦c❧❦c❧

Vol. III. Page 126.

An old man appeared at the bar. I atteft, fays he, that I was ill-treated by the revolutionary committee, becaufe I requefted the releafe of a young girl who was entirely innocent. The committee told me that I had no bufinefs to meddle with any fuch people. My nephew and my fon-in-law were fhot for no crime whatever; and, adds the old man, I had the grief to fee my own children dragged from my houfe to the fatal lighters. One of them made an attempt to efcape from the hands of his barbarous executioners, was caught and fhot.

❦c❧❦c❧❦c❧❦c❧❦c❧

I dare fay the reader is ready to weep for this poor diftreffed father; but let him referve his tears for more worthy objects. This old man was a murderer like the reft, and his own family had fallen into the pit he had dug for another. Yes, reader, this grey headed, ferocious old tyger, who complains of the cruelties of others, ends his evidence by accufing Carrier, even Carrier, of having fhown an act of mercy!—I ac‑ cufe him, (fays the hoary affaffin (PAGE 26) of being *no patriot*, fince he *did not execute* the wife of Templorie, whom I informed againft as an emigrant.

* * *

VOL. IV. PAGE 148.

Juget, a judge at Nantz, reads, from the regifter of his tribunal, an order of Carrier to fend thirty-fix men, twenty women, and four children, to be fhot, without being heard or tried. This was accordingly done.

* * *

VOL. IV. PAGE 148.

Poupon depofes, that he was witnefs of a drowning, when the company of Marat went and dragged fick perfons from the hofpital in order to make up a lighter full.—Some of thefe perfons, adds the wit‑

nefs, could fcarcely crawl along, and I faw
thefe murderers beat them moft cruelly with
great fticks, crying, along with you, b—gers!
march! march! we will give you fweet air
enough now.—Others they dragged along
by the hair of the head, till they got them
on board the lighter.—All this time, fays
the witnefs, the conductors of the expedition kept hollowing out, come, come, my
lads, be quick! along with the b—gers!
the tide falls apace: there is no time to be
loft.

Vol. IV. Page 151.

Seginel, one of the company of Marat,
informs the tribunal, that Goullin and Chaux
conducted fome of the company, one day,
to the houfe of Carrier. When we came,
fays this under cut-throat, into the prefence
of the reprefentative of the people, our conductors told him we were good lads, citizens
on whom he might rely. So much the better, fays Carrier, adding, depend on it,
my boys, if you do your duty like good
b—gers, the Republic, which is never ungrateful, will pay you well.

While we were there, fays the witnefs,
Lambertye came, and went into another

room with Carrier. Goullin afked Grand
Maifon who that man was. He is a fecond
Marat, replied the latter, and is now, without doubt, receiving orders to communicate to us.

*﹥﹥ ﹤﹤·﹥﹥ ﹤﹤·﹥﹥ ﹤﹤·﹥﹥ ﹤﹤·

Marat.

The name of Marat has been fo often
mentioned, it may not be improper, or out
of place, to give the reader here fome account of that famous cut-throat.

Before the revolution, he was an obfcure beggarly fellow, that was daily liable
to be brought before the officer of police
to give an account of the manner in which
he got his bread. But, when this grand
event took place; when murderers were
wanted in every quarter of the country, he
began to cut a figure on the fcene. He
publifhed a gazette, in which he inculcated
the neceffity of lopping off the heads of
thoufands at a time, and of watering, as
he called it, the tree of liberty with the
blood of the ariftocrats, as the only means
of rendering it fruitful.

Thefe, and fuch like fentiments, recommended him to the notice of his country,

K 3

men; he obtained their confidence, and was one of the *organizers* (to ufe a French term) of the maffacres of the 2d and 3d of September, 1792, of which I have fpoken in the firft chapter of this work. On this occafion he was an actor alfo, and is faid to have cut above fifty throats with his own hands.

It would have been fomething unjuft if a man like this had been forgotten, when the Convention was to affemble. He was not. The people of Paris, who had been eye-witneffes of his merit, chofe him for one of their reprefentatives; and he was faithful in the execution of his truft; for he never talked about any thing but of throats to cut, ftabbing, and guillotining.

His career, however, was but fhort. His own neck was not made of iron: a defperate woman, who had adopted his principles, rufhed into his apartment, and delivered the world of one of the greateft monfters that ever difhonoured it.

There was fomething horrible in the look of this villain. He was very fhort and thick, had a black beard afcending nearly to the extreme corners of his eyes. This beard was ufually long, and his hair fhort, fticking up like briftles. He had ever been dirty, and it may be imagined, that the fafhions of a revolution which has made it

a *crime* to be *well-dreſſed*, had not improved
his appearance : in ſhort, he was at the very
beſt, a moſt difguſting mortal, and, therefore, when he came out of the priſon of
Là Force, all covered with filth and gore,
wielding a piſtol in one hand and a dagger
in the other, no wonder that even the ſan-
guinary mob ran back for fear.

❀⟨⟩✦✠⟨⟩✦✠❀✠⟨⟩✦✠⟨⟩✦✠❀⟨⟩✦

Charlotte Cordée.

As I have entered on a digreſſion, I will
continue it a little longer, to give the reader
an account of the execution of Charlotte
Cordée, the young woman that murdered
Marat.

She was not what is commonly called an
ariſtocrat ; but a patriot of another faction
than Marat. She was, as it is ſaid, employed by the party of Briſſot, who, from
the accompliſhments of Marat, were afraid
that he would totally engroſs the favour and
affections of the people. Poor Charlotte
received her reward on the ſcaffold ; and a
very juſt reward too ; but there is ſome-
thing ſo ſhocking in the behaviour of her
executioner, that it ought not to be omitted
in a collection of this kind.

She was a beautiful young woman; extremely fair; and, in any other country, would have brought tears of compaffion from the fpectators. The executioner, after having cut off her head, feized it by the fine long hair, and, holding it up by one hand, the brutal ruffian gave her a flap in the face with the other, " The bitch " blufhes," cried he, " at any rate." This trait of hangman wit excited the favage mirth of the populace. *

We muft now return to Nantz, where we fhall find the revolutionary committee employed in writing to their friends at Paris.

Before they began to drown and fhoot by hundreds, they had feized on the perfons of one hundred and thirty-two of the moft opulent men in the city, and fent them off to Paris to be tried as *fufpected perfons.* It appears, from the whole courfe of the evidence on this head, that the detachment of patriots who conducted them, were, if any pretence could be found, to murder them all by the way. This, however, did not

* It is fomething very remarkable that her face, fevered from the body, fhould blufh; but it is a real fact, as appears from an effay lately republifhed at Philadelphia, in Gatreau's Gazette.

happen. The prifoners arrived fafe at Paris, and the committee were obliged to have recourfe to other means, to prevent their return. The one that they adopted was to infure their guillotining at Paris; and, for this purpofe, they wrote to the revolutionary commitee of the fection of Lepelletier.— Their letter is, and I hope it ever will be, a curiofity in this country. I fhall give it a literal tranflation, that the reader may be able to do juftice to the memory of the writers.

❧❀❧❀❧❀❧❀❧❀

VOL. IV. PAGE 179.

Nantz, this 5th of Pluviofe.

Liberty, Equality or Death.

Citizens,

The people of Nantz, whom we have fent to Paris, are big villains, all marked with the feal of reprobation, and known for counter-revolutionifts. We are collecting proofs againft them, which we fhall fend, when the bundle is made up, to the revolutionary judges. In the mean time, we *denounce* to you, Julienne, who has *officioufly* taken upon him the defence of thefe *uncivic vermin.*

From the moment the revolutionary committee was inftalled, fays *Benét*, the im-
prifonments began ; and they augmented
daily. They were all dictated by animofity,
hatred, or avarice. To fuch a degree did
terror prevail, that every man trembled for
his life.

For my part, fays the witnefs, my refolution was taken. I always went with two
loaded piftols in my pockets : one for the
villain that fhould offer to feize me, and the
other for myfelf. Cruel expectation for a
man who had a fmall helplefs family. But
I had feen fix hundred men at one time
plunged into the water, and had been a
witnefs of fhootings amounting to three
thoufand fix hundred perfons at the Gigan :
after this what could any man hope for ?

There is reafon to believe that Carrier
meant to murder the whole city ; for, before his journey to Paris, he told one of the
women whom he kept, and *whofe hufband
he had put to death*, that he would make
Nantz remember the name of Carrier : do
not fear, *my dear*, faid he, all my friends
fhall follow me ; but as for the city it fhall
he deftroyed (PAGE 219.)

I was one day, adds the fame witnefs, fent by Bowin to fee fome bodies buried, that were left on the public fquare. There were upwards of thirty women, all naked, and expofed with the moft horrible indecency.

Fontaine. I went one day to a prifon where a great many women and children were confined. My bufinefs was to deliver provifions to thefe people; but I found neither fire, lights, nor any thing elfe. I called for a candle, in order to enter this abode of horror. The prifoners were lying here and there on the bare boards, though it was extremely cold.

In a fecond vifit that I made here, I found the poor unhappy creatures in a worfe fituation than before. I faw a woman lying dead, and a fucking child, at a little diftance from her, wallowing about in the filth. It's little face was abfolutely covered with ordure. I gave the keeper ten livres to take care of this helplefs infant, till I could find a nurfe, but when I came for it, it was gone; and Dumey told me, that the Englifh prifoners had taken the child with a promife to do well by it.

It feems, from the evidence of feveral wit neffes, that, while thefe villains were butcher ing, or ftifling their own countrymen, the took care to treat foreign prifoners wit fome fort of humanity. This diftinctio fully proves, that they acted by authority of the Convention. But we fhall this fo in conteftibly proved by-and-by, that the re mark is hardly neceffary here.

✦❁✦❁✦✦❁✦✦❁✦

VOL. IV. PAGE 210.

I faw, fays the fame witnefs, a man, named Gorgo, come and afk for a little boy, that he faid he had obtained permiffion to take. The child was found behind a bundle of ftuff, where he had run to hide upon hearing voices. Gorgo brought him to the door-way, and made him *dance and fing*.

I have felected this laft fact to fhow to what a pitch of obduracy, of unfeeling in-difference, thefe people were arrived. A thoufand volumes could not paint their fa-miliarity with fcenes of horror fo well as this trifling circumftance of making a child dance and fing, at the entrance of a cavern of defpair, a human flaughter-houfe, where perhaps his own parents were at that moment groaning their laſt.

Vol. IV. Page 210.

Chaux, one of the criminals, informs the tribunal, that he was diſpatched from Nantz to wait on Carrier, during his ſtay at Paris. He told me, ſays Chaux, that he did not like Philippes, and that we ſhould guillotine him, at my return.—I have communicated, ſays Carrier, all our proceedings to the National Convention.— You muſt not, adds he, try Lambertye ; he is too precious a patriot. I intend to ſend for him here, and preſent him to the committee of *public preſervation (ſalut public)* who will not leave him unrecompenſed for his ſervices.

Jicquieau ſays (Page 273.) that Lambertye was the *chief murderer.*—This it was that made him a *precious patriot*, and a man worthy of reward from a committee of the National Convention.

This witneſs adds : when the committee of Nantz was firſt inſtalled, a deputation was ſent to Carrier, to let him know that no proofs could be made out againſt Jom-

L

ard.   The reprefentative of the people, feeing the deputation enter, cried out, what are all thefe b—gers come here for ? When he heard our bufinefs, to hell with you, fays he, you fool. But, feeming to grow a little calm, he called me back into his room, and threatened to throw me out of the window. At laft, fays the witnefs, he told me there were other means befides guillotining; you have only, fays he, to fend Jomard into the country, and have him difpatched fecretly.

Here we behold a member of the National Convention of France; one of thofe *philofophical* legiflators, who call themfelves the *enlighteners* of the univerfe.   This bafe, this cowardly cut-throat, this affaffin-general, is one of thofe men, whom we have been told are to *regenerate* mankind, and to eftablifh a fyftem of univerfal *humanity!*

The following traits will depict the leaders in the French Revolution.

VOL. IV. PAGE 273.

Robin, fays a witnefs, was one of the accomplices of Carrier.   This Robin, one day, fhowed his fabre all ftained with blood, faying at the fame time, with this I chopped off fixty of the heads of the ariftocrats that we drowned laft night.

Vol. IV. Page 209.

Fontaine informs the tribunal, that he was one night at the *Entrepot*. Here, fays the witnefs, I faw a little man (this afterwards appears to have been Fouquet) wearing pantaloons, and a liberty cap. It is I, faid the little monfter, who conduct all the drownings; it is I who give the word of command to pull up the plugs; nothing is done without my orders. If you will come along with me, continued he, I will fhow you how to feed upon the flefh of an ariftocrat; I will regale you with the brains of thofe rafcals.—I trembled, fays the witnefs, and got away from this canibal as foon as I could.

Vol. IV. Page 276.

Fontbonne informs the tribunal, that he was one day invited to a dinner, in a pleafure garden belonging to Ducrois. Carrier and O'Sullivan were of the party. The converfation turned on the bodily ftrength of certain perfons, when O'Sullivan obferved; " yes, there was my brother, who was devilifh ftrong, particularly in the neck, for the executioner was obliged to give him the fecond ftroke with the *national razor*, before he could get his head off."

The witnefs adds, O'Sullivan told us, that he was going to drown a man much ftronger than himfelf; that the man refifted, but was knocked down; then, fays O'Sullivan, I took my knife and ftruck him, as butchers do the fheep.

Guedon informs the tribunal (Vol. IV. page 277.) that he was at the fame dinner mentioned by Fontbonne. I was feated, fays this witnefs, by the fide of O'Sullivan; and, during the repaft, he held up his knife to me, and faid, this is excellent to cut a man's throat with; adding, that it had already done him good fervice in that way. He called on Robin as a witnefs of his bravery, and told us the manner in which he proceeded.—I had remarked, fays O'Sullivan, that the butchers killed their fheep by plunging their knife in underneath the ear; fo, when I had a mind to kill a prifoner, I came up to him, and, clapping him on the fhoulder in a jocular way, pointed to fome object that he was obliged to turn his head to fee; the moment he did this, I had my knife through his neck.

This O'Sullivan, in his defence, fays,. that, as to his brother,. he was an enemy of the Republic.. When he faw,. fays this human butcher, that there was no hope for him, he came and threw himfelf into my; arms; but, *like a good republican*, I gave him up to the guillotine.

❮❮❬❯❯ ❮❮❬❯❯ ❮❮❬❯❯ ❮❮❬❯❯.

VOL. II. PAGE 281.

A witnefs fays, that Goullin beat his own father with a ftick, when the old man was on his death-bed; and adds, that his father died in two hours after.

This fame Goullin (VOL. II. PAGE 253) faid in the tribune of his club, take care not to admit among you moderate men, half patriots. Admit none but real revolution-ifts; none but patriots who have the courage to drink a glafs of human blood, warm from the veins.

Goullin, fo far from denying this, fays before the tribunal (PAGE 254) that he glo-ries in thinking like Marat, who would will-ingly have quenched his thirft with the blood of the ariftocrats.

L 3

I shall conclude this chapter, this frightful tragedy exhibited at Nantz, with the relation of a few traits of diabolical cruelty, which not only surpass all that the imagination has hitherto been able to conceive, but even all that has been related in this volume. I have classed these facts together, that the indignant reader may tear out the leaf, and commit it to the flames.

Yes (says the author of *La Conjuration*, page 160) yes; we have seen a representative of the people, a member of the National Convention, tie four children, the eldest of which was but sixteen years of age, to the four posts of the guillotine. while the blood of their father and mother streamed on the scaffold, and even dropped on their heads.

Vol. V. Page 36.

Lailet deposes, that Deron came to the popular society with a man's ear, pinned to the national cockade, which he wore in his cap. He went about, says the witness, with a pocket full of these ears, which he made the female prisoners kiss.

Vol. II. Page 267.

Many of the generals in La Vendee, says Forget, made it their glory to imitate the horrid butchers at Nantz. They committed unheard of cruelties and indecencies. General Duquefnoy murdered feveral infants at the breaft, and afterwards attempted to lie with the mothers.

This is the infernal monfter that ftiled himfelf the butcher of the Convention, and that faid, nothing hurt him fo much as not being able to ferve them in the capacity of executioner.

Vol. II. Page 122.

I faw, fays *Girault*, about three or four hundred perfons drowned. There were women of all ages amongft them; fome were big with child, and of thefe feveral were delivered in the very lighters, among water and mud. This moft fhocking circumftance, their groans, their heart-piercing fhrieks, excited no compaffion. They with the fruit of their conjugal love, went to bottom together.

***

VOL. II. PAGE 153.

Coron. A woman going to be drowned, was taken in child birth ; fhe was in the act of delivery, when the horrid villains tore the child from her body, ftuck it on the point of a bayonet, and thus carried it to the river.

A fourth of thefe, our reprefentatives, (fays the author of *La Conjuration,* PAGE 162) a fourth (great God! my heart dies within me) a fourth, ripped open the wombs of the mothers, tore out the palpitating embryo, to deck the point of a pike of liberty and equality.

***

The reader's curiofity may, perhaps, lead him to wifh to know the whole number of perfons put to death at Nantz ; but, in this, it would be difficult to gratify him. I have been able to obtain but *five volumes* of the trial, which make only a part of that work; probably the laſt volume may contain an exact account as to numbers. The deaths muſt, however, have been immenſe, ſince a witneſs depoſes (Vol. III. Page 55) to the drowning of *nine thouſand* perſons; and another witneſs (Vol. II. Page 253) atteſts, that *ſeven thouſand five hundred* were ſhot *en maſſe*.

The number of bodies thrown into the river Loire, which is half the width of the Delaware at Philadelphia, was ſo conſiderable, that the municipal officers found it neceſſary to iſſue a proclamation (Vol. V. Page 70), *forbidding the uſe of its waters.*

It has been generally computed that the number of perſons, belonging to this unfortunate city and its environs, who were drowned, ſhot *en maſſe*, guillotined, and ſtifled or ſtarved in priſon, amounted to about *forty* thouſand. And this computation is corroborated by the author of *La Conjuration*, who ſays (Page 159), The number of perſons murdered in the ſouth of France, during the ſpace of a very few months, is reckoned at a hundred thouſand. The bodies thrown into the Loire are innumerable. Carrier alone put to death *more than forty thouſand*, including men, women and children.

It appears, then, that thefe bloody revolt tionifts, who ftiled themfelves the friends c freedom and of mankind, deftroyed, in on city of France, a population equal to tha of the capital of the United States.

C H A P. IV.

acts from several works, proving that the cruelties related in the preceding chapters were authorized, or approved of by the National Assemblies.

AFTER having led the reader through such rivers of blood, it seems indifensibly necessary to insert a few facts, ıowing by whose authority that blood was ıilt; for, it could answer no good purpose ı, excite his detestation, without directing it ıwards the proper object.

When the French first began that career f, insurrection, robbery and murder, which ſſumed the name of a Revolution, the peole of this country, or at least the most umerous part of them, felt uncommon nxiety for its success. The people were eceived; but the deception was an agreeble one; the word *Revolution* had of itself ery great charms, but when that of *Liber-ı* was added to it, it could not fail of exiting enthusiasm. This enthusiasm was, ineed, nearly general; and this alone was a ıfficient inducement for the public prints to ıecome the partizans of Condorcet and Miabeau. All the avenues to truth were as once barred up; and, though the revolutionists every day changed their creed, though one revolving moon saw them make and break their oaths, all was amply atoned for by their being engaged in a Revolution.

As the Revolution advanced the enthusiasm increased; but from the moment that the French nation declared itself a *Republic*, this enthusiasm was changed to madness. All the means by which this change of government was to be accomplished were totally overlooked; nothing was talked or dreamed of but the enfranchisement of the world; the whole universe was to become a' republic, or be annihilated; and happy was he who could bawl loudest about a certain something, called *liberty and equality*.

During this political madness, however, now and then a trait of shocking barbarity, in spite of all the endeavours of the public papers, burst in upon us, and produced a lucid interval; but these intervals have never yet been of long duration; because every subterfuge, that interested falsehood can devise, has been made use of to give our abhorrence a direction contrary to that which it ought to have taken. We have heard Briffot, Danton, Marat, and Robespierre, all accused in their turns of shedding innocent blood; but the *National Affembly* itself, they tell us, has ever remained worthy of our admiration. The poor unfuccefsful agents of this terrible divan have been devoted to execration, as tyrants, while their employers have been, and are yet held up to us as the friends of liberty and the lovers of mankind.

Without further remark, I fhall add fuch facts as, I imagine, will enable every reader to judge for himfelf.

To begin with the conftituent affembly; one proof of their approving of murder will fuffice. They honoured with the title of *vanquifhers*, a blood-thirfty mob, who, after having taken two men prifoners, cruelly maffacred them, and carried their heads about the ftreets of Paris on a pike. *See Rabaud's Hiftory of the French Revolution*, page 106.

The fecond Affembly, when they received advices of the murders of Jourdan and his affociates at Avignon, as mentioned in the firft chapter of this work, threatened the member who communicated the news, becaufe he had called the murderers *brigands*, and not *patriots. See La Gazette Univerfelle* for the month of May 1792.—And, how did this Affembly behave, when informed of the maffacres in the prifons of Paris, during the firft days of September, 1792 ? *Tallien* (of whom we have lately heard fo

M

much) came to the National Affembly, and
informed them of the murdering in the following remarkable words : " The commif-
" miffaries have done all they could to pre-
" vent the *diforders* (the maffacreing the pri-
" foners is what he calls *diforders*) but they
" have not been able to ftop the, in fome
" fort, *juft vengeance* of the people."—The
Affembly heard this language very quietly,
and Doctor Moore, from whofe journal (page
178.) the fact is taken, makes an apology
for the Affembly, by faying that they were
overawed; but it has fince fully appeared,
that the leading members were the very perfons who contrived the maffacre, with the
aid of Petion, Manuel, and Marat.—It is a
well known fact, recorded by the Abbé
Barruel (page 334.) that *Louvet*, one of the
members of the prefent Affembly, gave, the
day after the September maffacre, an order
on the public treafury, in the following
words : " *On fight, pay to the four bearers*
" *each twelve livres, for aiding in the dif-*
" *patching of the priefts at the prifon of St.*
" *Firmin*."—Louvet was, at the time of
writing this note on demand for murderer's
wages, a *legiflator*; and I cannot help remarking here, that a printer of a news-
paper in the United States has lately boafted,
that this Louvet, " now prefident of the
firft Affembly on earth," fays our printer,

was *the editor of a Gazette!*—People should
be cautious how they boast of relationship
with the legislators in that country of equality.

As it will no longer be pretended, I sup-
pose, that this second Assembly disapproved
of the murders that were committed under
their reign, I will now turn to the third
Assembly, which we commonly call a Convention. And, not to tire the reader with
proofs of what is self evident, I shall confine
myself to an extract or two from the trial of
Carrier and the revolutionary committee of
Nantz.

Vol. V. Page 49.

It is time, says Goulin, to tear aside the
veil. The representatives Bourbotte and
Bo knew all about the drownings and shootings; and Bo even said to Huchet, in
speaking of the members of the revolutionary committee, that it was *not for the murders* that they were to be tried.

After this the counsellor for the committee asks this citizen Bo, what was the real
motive for bringing the committee to trial;
and the other confesses, that it was for their
having *misapplied the treasures* taken from

the prisoners. He pretends (page 60) though he had taken the place of Carrier at Nantz, and though the water of the river could not be drank, on account of the dead bodies that were floating on it; though a hundred or two of ditches had been dug to put the people into that were shot, and though the city was filled with cries and lamentations; notwithstanding all this, he pretends that he could say nothing, for certain, *about the murders.*

This representative Bo (page 83) is convicted of having himself justified the conduct of the committee and of Carrier.

Carrier, in his defence, says, that he had done no more than *his duty,* and that *the Convention had been regularly informed of every thing.* They complain now, says he (page 119, *of shootings en masse, as if the same had not been done at Angers, Saumur, Laval, and every where else.*)

A witness (Vol. 5, Page 60.) informs the tribunal, that he, who was himself a member of the Convention, *had informed that body of all the horrors that were committed at Nantz,* and particularly of the *massacres of women and children.*

The author of *La Conjuration,* so often quoted says (page 162.) When the bloody Carrier wrote to the Convention that he was dispatching hundreds at a time by means of lighters with plugs in the bottom, Carrier was not blamed; on the contrary, he was *repeatedly applauded*, as being the author of *an invention that did honour to his country!*

But, what need have we of thefe proofs? What other teftimony do we want, than that contained in their own murderous decrees? Let any one caft his eye on the oppofite page; let him there behold the fcene that was daily exhibited before the windows of their hall, and then let him fay whether they delighted in murder or not. Blood is their element, as water is that of the finny race.

One thing, however, remains to be accounted for; and that is, how fo great a part of the nation were led to butcher each other; how they were brought to that pitch of brutal fanguinary ferocity, which we have feen fo amply difplayed in the preceding Chapters. This is what, with the reader's indulgence, I fhall now agreeable to my promife, endeavour to explain.

M 3

AN

INSTRUCTIVE ESSAY,

Tracing all the horrors of the French Revolution to their real caufes, the licentious Politics and infidel Philofophy of the prefent Age.

THAT the French were an amiable people the whole civilized world has given abundant teftimony, by endeavouring to imitate them. There was not a nation in Europe but had, in fome degree, adopted their language and their fafhions; and all thofe individuals, belonging even to their haughty rival enemy, who travelled in their country, were led by an involuntary impulfe into an imitation of their manners.

The prominent feature in their national character was, it is true, *levity*; but, though levity and ferocioufnefs may, and often do, meet in the fame perfon, no writer, that I recollect, had ever accufed the French of being cruel. If we are to judge of their

difpofition by their national fports and en-
tertainments, we fhall find no room to draw
a conclufion againft their humanity. Thefe
cruel diverfions, where men become the
bullies of brute creatures, and laugh at feeing them goad, and bite, and tear each
other to pieces, were never known in France.
Even in their theatrical performances a dead
body was never exhibited on the fcene:
fuch a fpectacle was thought to be too much
for the feelings of the audience. The works
of their favourite authors generally breathe
the greatelt tendernefs and humanity. The
nation that could produce, and admire, a
Marmontel and a Racine, could not be naturally bloody-minded.

" To kinder fkies, where gentler manners reign,
" I turn,—and France difplays her bright domain.
" Gay fprightly land of mirth and focial eafe,
" Pleas'd with thyfelf, whom all the world can
                               [pleafe:
" How often have I led thy fportive choir,
" With tunelefs pipe befide the murm'ring Loire!
" Where fhading elms along the margin grew,
" And, frefhen'd from the wave, the zephyr flew;
" And haply, tho' my harfh touch falt'ring ftill,
" But mock'd all tune, and marr'd the dancer's fkill,
" Yet would the village praife my wond'rous pow'r,
" And dance forgetful of the noon-tide hour!

" Alike all ages. Dames of ancient days
" Have led their child'ren thro' the mirthful maze,
" And the gay Grand fire, fkill'd in geftic lore,
" Has frifked beneath the burden of threefcore.
  " So bleft a life thefe thoughtlefs realms difplay;
" Thus idly bufy rolls their world away :
" Theirs are thofe arts which mind to mind endear;
" For honour forms the focial temper here."

Thefe verfes, extracted from the moft
elegant of poems, dictated by the beft of
hearts, contain the jufteft character of the
French nation, that I have ever yet feen.
To this character I am ready to fubfcribe :
for, I too have been charmed with their
gentle manners, and their focial eafe : I too
have felt the power of thofe arts which endear mind to mind : I have been a witnefs
of their urbanity, their refpectful deference
and attention to the fofter fex, their pater-
nal tendernefs, and their veneration for old
age.

Whence, then, the mighty, the dreadful change ? What is it that has transformed
a great portion of this airy humane people
into a horde of fullen affaffins ? What is
it that has converted thefe thoughlefs
realms; this gay fprightly land of mirth,
this bright domain, into a gloomy wilder-
nefs watered with rivers of human blood ?
This ought to be the great object of our en-

quiries : this ought to fix all our attention.
Without determining this point, we can
draw no profit from the preceding relation,
and without attempting it, I fhould have
undertaken the unpleafant tafk of holding
the French people up to reproach and deteftation to no manner of purpofe.

It has been afferted, again and again, by
the partizans of the French revolution, that
all the crimes which have difgraced it, are
to be afcribed to the hoftile operations of
their enemies. They have told us, that,
had not the Auftrians and Pruffians been on
their march to Paris, the prifoners would
not have been maffacred, on the 2d and
3d of September, 1792. But, can we
poffibly conceive how the murder of 8,000
poor prifoners, locked up and bound, could
be neceffary to the defence of a Capital,
containing a million of inhabitants ? Can
we believe that the fabres of the affaffins
would not have been more effectually employed againft the invaders, than againft defencelefs priefts and women. The deluded
populace were told not " to leave the wolves
" in the fold while they went to attack
" thofe that were without." But thefe
wolves, if they were fuch, were in prifon ;
were under a guard an hundred thoufand
times as ftrong as themfelves, and could

have been deftroyed at a moment's warning. There is fomething fo abominably cowardly in this juftification, that it is even more bafe than the crime. Suppofe that a hundred thoufand men had marched from Paris, to make head againft the Auftrians and Pruffians, there were yet nine hundred thoufand left to guard the unhappy wretches that were tied hand and foot. Where could be the neceffity of maffacreing them! Where could be the neceffity of hacking them to pieces, tearing out their bowels, and biting their hearts?

Subfequent events have fully proved, that it was not danger that produced thefe bloody meafures: for, we have ever feen the revolutionifts moft cruel in times of their greateft fecurity. Their butcheries at Lyons and in its neighbourhood did not begin till they were completely triumphant. It was then, at the moment when they had no retaliation to fear, that they commenced their bloody work. Carrier, lolling at his eafe, fent the victims to death by hundreds. The blood never flowed from the guillotine in fuch torrents, as at the very time when their armies were driving their enemies before them in every direction.

It has been faid in the Britifh Houfe of Commons, that the maffacres in France ought to be attributed to the Allied Powers. " You hunt them like wild beasts, and " then you complain of them for being " ferocious." How this hunting could drive the French to butcher one another, I cannot see ; but if it was a justifiable reason for them, it might certainly be applied with much more justice to their enemies ; for these have been oftener obliged to fly than the French. The revolutionary armies have over-run an extent of territory equal to one third of their own country : the Savoyards, the Germans, the Flemings, the Dutch, the Spaniards, and the English, have been obliged to fly before them ; but we have heard of no massacres among these people. The French most unmercifully put to death eight thousand of their country people, who were in the prisons of Paris, and, as an ex-cuse for this, they tell us that the Duke of Brunswick had invaded the province of Champagne ; but they themselves have over-run all the United Netherlands, and even taken possession of the capital ; and we have not heard that the Dutch have, as yet, been guilty of a single massacre. They have found but one place in all their ca-reer, where the people could be prevailed on to erect a guillotine, and that was at Geneva. Here their army was more numerous than the whole population of the ftate, and therefore their fyftem was fully adopted; yet even here, among this little debafed and tyranized people, there were to be found no villains infamous enough to imitate their mafters in murdering women and children. That was a fpecies of flaughter referved for the French nation alone.

The French revolution has been compared to that of America, and I have heard fome men, calling themfelves Americans, who have not been afhamed to fay, that as great cruelties were committed in this country as in that. I would now afk thefe men, who are fo anxious to be thought as bloody as the fans-culotte French, if they can give me one inftance of the Americans murdering their towns-men at the approach of the enemy? When the Britifh army fucceeded that of the Congrefs at Philadelphia, did the continental troops murder all the Tories before they quitted the City? Can thefe generous friends of the French revolution tell us of any maffacres that took place in this country? Did they ever -hear of women and children being drowned and fhot by hundreds? Seven years of civil war defolated thefe ftates, but the blood of one fingle woman or child never ftained the earth.

If the doctrine be admitted, if a people be juftifiable in entering on a feries of maffacres the inftant they are preffed by an enemy from without, what fafety can there be for any of us ? If a declaration of war is to unfheath the daggers of all the affaffins in the community, civil fociety is the greateft curfe that ever fell upon mankind. Much better and fafer were it for us to feparate, and prowl about like favages, nay like beafts, than to live thus, in continual trepidation, in continual fear for our throats.

There is fomething fo exceedingly cowardly and ridiculous in this juftification, that even the French revolutionifts are afhamed of it. They have recourfe to another ftill more difhonourable, it is true, but lefs cowardly. They tell us, that all the affaffins in France have been in the pay of Great Britain; or, to make ufe of their own expreffion, have been excited to action by the " *gold of Pitt.*"

As I wifh to advance nothing without the beft poffible authority, I fhall here infert a paffage on this fubject, taken from a Gazette publifhed at Philadelphia by one *Gatreau,* and at the prefs of *Moreau de St. Mery,* who was a member of the conftituent affembly of France.

N

The intention of the piece evidently is to juftify the French charaçter, or rather the charaçter of the French revolutionifts, by attributing the horrid deeds thefe latter have committed, to fome caufe other than their own difpofitions and anarchical principles. To avoid all cavil with refpeçt to the authenticity of the extraçt, and the correçtnefs of the tranflation, I will firft give it in French, and then in Englifh, obferving, for the further fatisfaçtion of the reader, that he may find the piece entire in the Gazette above-mentioned, of the fourth of February, 1796.

" Quel homme éclairé par l'expérience,
" nieroit aujhurd'hui, que, de la tête de
" Pitt font fortis tous les crimes qui fefoient
" abhorrer la Revolution par ceux-là meme
" qui en adoroient les principes; que, c'eft
" au foyer de la jaloufie et de la haine An-
" gloife, que s'allumèrent les torches, que
" fe forgèrent les poignards, qui ont fait un
" monceau de cendres et de fang des plus
" belles poffeffions du monde?—Quel génie
" malfaifant créa les factions impies, fan-
" guinaires ou ambitieufes, qui devoient
" anéantir la France, au du moins la re-
" placer fous le joug, fi la providence ne
" déconcertoit pas toujours les complots de
" l'iniquité?—Le génie infernal du miniftre
" Anglois.—C'eft avec l'or de fes victimes

" de l'Inde qu'il payoit le fang François,
" verfé à grands flots à Paris, dans les de-
" partemens, aux frontières et dans les co-
" lonies."

" What man, enlightened by experience,
" will now deny, that, from the head of
" Pitt have come all the crimes which have
" rendered the Revolution deteftable in the
" eyes of even thofe who adored its princi-
" ples; that, it was Englifh jealouly and
" hatred that lighted the flames, and fhar-
" pened the poignards, which have re-
" duced the fineft poffeffions in the world
" to a heap of afhes and blood?—What
" evil genius created the impious, fangui-
" nary and ambitious factions, that were to
" annihilate France; or, at leaft, bend it
" again beneath the yoke, if Providence
" had not difconcerted the plans of iniqui-
" ty?—The infernal genius of the Eng-
" lifh Minifter. It was with the gold,
" drawn from his victims in India, that he
" paid for the French blood, which has
" flowed in rivers at Paris, in the depart-
" ments, on the frontiers, and in the colo-
" nies.

This is an *important*, and were it not fo
very hackneyed and thread-bare, I would
call it a " *precious confeff:n.*" Here we fee
a Frenchman, a partizan of, and perhaps
an actor in, the revolution, endeavouring

to wipe away the ſtain on its principles, by aſcribing all the horrors thoſe principles have produced, to the gold diſtributed among the revolutioniſts by the Engliſh miniſter. The cruelties that have been committed were not, then, neceſſary to the eſtabliſhment of a free government; they were not the effect of irritation, of anarchical confuſion, of vindictive retaliation; they were not the natural conſequence of a long-oppreſſed people's breaking their chains and riſing on their tyrants; all theſe excuſes (which I muſt allow were ſilly enough) are at once done away by this new juſtification; for, we are here told, in ſo many words, that the French people have ſhed rivers of each other's blood, in every part of their dominions, purely for the love—not of *liberty*, but of *the gold of Pitt*.

There is ſuch a natural connection between the meaſures of the ſeveral National Aſſemblies and the maſſacres that were the immediate conſequence of them, that it is impoſſible to effect a ſeparation without the utmoſt violence to all manner of reaſoning and truth. If it was the gold of Pitt that paid for all the French blood that has been ſpilled, it muſt have been that gold that paid for the inhuman murder of Meſſrs. Launy and Fleſſel, and it muſt have been that gold which induced the conſtituent aſfembly to fanction the murder, by giving the affaffins of thefe gen-lemen the title of *heroes* and *conquerors*, and by inftituting a national feftival in their honour.

The Revolution was begun, and has hitherto been maintained by the fhedding of innocent blood; therefore, if it was the gold of Pitt that paid for that blood, it is to the gold of Pitt that the revolution is to be afcribed, and not to that patriotic fpi it and love of liberty, with which we have been fo long amufed. In the fifth chapter of this work, it is inconteftibly proved, that the feveral National Affemblies authorifed, or approved of all the maffacres which have difgraced their country; if, then, thefe maffacres were paid for by Mr. Pitt, muft we not inevitably conclude that the National Affemblies were in the fame pay? If Mr. Pitt paid for the blood of the family of Bourbon, for that of the king's guards, of the nobility, the clergy, the bankers, the merchants, in fhort, of all the rich or ariftocrats, as they are called, it was Mr. Pitt who deftroyed the monarchy: it was he who caufed France to be called a Republic, and who gave rife to the doctrine of *equality*. Thofe, therefore, who talk of the gold of Pitt, muft ceafe all their fulfome culogiums on thefe gallant republicans; for, if they are to have a republic, it will, according to their own confeſſions, be the work of the Engliſh Miniſter.

This vindication, throwing the blame on the gold of Pitt, amply participates in the misfortune of all the vindications that have lately appeared amongſt us; that is, it takes up a bad cauſe, and makes it worſe. The reader will certainly feel, with me, an inexpreſſible indignation at a people, who, becauſe an hoſtile army was on their frontiers, could be prevailed on to butcher thouſands upon thouſands of their innocent countrymen; who could cut the throats of their fathers and mothers, rip up the bowels of women with child, and carry about the trophies of their baſe and ſavage triumph on the points of their pikes and bayonets; but, what will be his feelings, what will contain his ſwelling heart, when he is told, that all this was undertaken and perpetrated for foreign gold? The revolutioniſts, by accuſing Mr. Pitt of being at the bottom of their maſſacres, do not perceive, without doubt, that they are heaping ten times ten-fold infamy on themſelves and their nation.

By alledging this influence of Britiſh gold, the writer I have above quoted reduces himſelf and the partizans of the revolution to a moſt diſtreſſing dilemma. He owns that rivers of French blood have flowed at Paris, in the departments, on the frontiers, and in the colonies; and he tells us, that this blood was paid for with the gold of Pitt. Now, admitting this to be true, this blood has been fhed, and this gold received, by *Frenchmen*. To what, then, will our author afcribe this fanguinary avarice? He muft either afcribe it to the *na'ural difpofition* of his countrymen; or, *a change* in that natural difpofition, *produced by the revolution*. It is uncertain which of thefe he may choofe, but it is very certain, choofe which he will, that he h is held up the character of his nation, or the principles of the revolution, to deteftation and abhorrence. This is the way he has juftified the French in the eyes of the people of this country. Infinitely better were it for fuch juftifiers to fuffer the prefs to reft in eternal inaction. All that a good Frenchman can do, is, to weep over the difgrace of his country; for, fo long as murder, horrid, barbarous, favage murder, fhall admit of no excufe, fo long fhall the actions of the French Revolutionifts remain unjuftifiable.

It is more than probable, that a writer of this ftamp might be willing to allow, that his countrymen were always naturally ferocious and bloody-minded, rather than confefs that this difpofition has been produced by the principles of the revolution: for, patriots of this kind are ever ready to facrifice the honour of their country to the fupport of their fyftems. But juftice demands from us to reject with difdain every fuch conclufion. We have feen the French people fprightly, beneficent, humane and happy; let us, now, follow them ftep by ftep into the awful oppofite, and fee for ourfelves, by what diabolical means the change has been effected.

The firft National Affembly had hardly affumed that title, when they difcovered an intention of overturning the government, which had been called together, and which their conftituents had enjoined them, to fupport, and of levelling all ranks and diftinctions among the different orders in the community. To this they were not led, as it had been fo falfely pretended, by their love of liberty and defire of feeing their country happy; but by envy, curfed envy, that will never let the fiery demagogue fleep in peace, while he fees a greater or richer than himfelf. It has been objected to this, that there were among the revolutionifts men who already enjoyed diftinguifhed honours; but it is forgotten at the fame time, that ambition will be at the top, or no where; that it will deftroy itfelf with the envied object, rather than act a fubaltern part. The motto of a demagogue is that of Milton's Satan : " rather reign in hell than ferve in heaven."

This tafk of deftruction was, however. an arduous one. To tear the complicated work of fourteen centuries to pieces at once, to renders honours difhonourable, and turn reverential awe into contempt and mockery, was not to be accomplifhed but by extraordinary means. It was evident that property muft change hands, that the beft blood of the nation muft flow in torrents, or the project muft fail. The affembly, to arm the multitude on their fide, broached the popular doctrine of *equality*. It was a neceffary part of the plan of thefe reformers to feduce the people to their fupport ; and fuch was the credulity of the unfortunate French, that they foon began to look on them as the oracles of virtue and wifdom, and believed themfelves raifed, by one fhort fentence iffued by thefe ambitious impoftors, from the ftate of *fubjects* to that of *fovereigns*.

" I punifhed" fays Solon, the Athenian law-giver,) " I punifhed with death all, " thofe afpiring difturbers of the common- " wealth, who, in order to domineer them- " felves, and lead the vulgar in their train, " pretended that all men were equal, and " fought to confound the different ranks in " fociety, by preaching up a chimerical

" equality, that never did or can exist." How happy would it have been for France, had there been some Solon, endued with wisdom and power enough to punish the political mountebanks of the Constituent Assembly! What dreadful carnage, what indelible disgrace, the nation would have escaped! Hardly had the word *equality* been pronounced, when the whole kingdom became a scene of anarchy and confusion. The name of liberty (I say the *name*, for the regenerated French have known nothing of it but the name.) The name of liberty had already half turned the heads of the people, and that of equality finished the work. From the moment it sounded in their ears, all that had formerly inspired respect, all that they had reverenced and adored, even began to excite contempt and fury. Birth, beauty, old age, all became the victims of a destructive equality, erected into a law by an Assembly of ambitious tyrants, who were ready to destroy every thing that crossed their way to absolute domination.

One of the immediate effects of the promulgation of this doctrine was the murder of Monsieur Foulon and his son-in-law Berthier, who, without so much as being charged with any crime, were taken by the people, conducted to Paris, and cruelly maſſacred. I will ſay nothing (ſays *Du Gour* in his eloquent *Memoire*, page 35) I will ſay nothing of the ſavage cruelties committed on Foulon and Berthier; I will not repreſent the bloody head of the father-in law, offered to the ſon to kiſs, prcſſed againſt his lips, and afterwards put under his feet; I will not repreſent the inhuman aſſaſſins ruſhing on Berthier, tearing out his heart, and placing it, quivering and ſtill palpitating, on the table of the town-hall, *before the magiſtrates* of the commune.—After this their heads were ſtuck on pikes, and the heart of Berthier on the point of a ſword. In this manner they were carried through the ſtreets, followed by the exulting populace (ſee *Rabaut's* Hiſtory of the French Revolution, page 117.) Nor let it be pretended that the Aſſembly could not prevent this ſhameful, this bloody deed. They had the abſolute command of Paris at the time, and had two hundred thouſand armed men ready to obey their nod. But the Aſſembly never oppoſed the murder of thoſe whom they looked upon as their enemies; nay, Rabaut, their partial hiſtorian (who was one of their body) even juſtifies the murder.

When the word *equality* found its way to the colonies it was only a ſignal for aſſaſſination. At Port-au-Prince the Chevalier de

Mauduit, a brave and generous officer, who
rendered effential fervices to this country
during the laft war, was mudered by his
own foldiers. The villains had the infolence
to order him to kneel down before them :
" No," faid he, like a foldier as he was,
" It fhall never be faid that Thomas Mau-
" duit bent his knee before a fet of fcoun-
" drels."—His head was cut off; he was
torn limb from limb; his bowels were trail-
ed along the ftreet, as butchers do thofe of
beafts in a flaughter houfe. The next morning the different members of his body, and
morfels of his flefh, were feen ftrewed about
oppofite his houfe, and his bloody and ghaftly
head placed on the ftep of the door-way.—
We know we have before our eyes the
proofs of what havock, diftrefs, and deftruction this deteftable word has fince produced
in the unfortunate ifland of St. Domingo.

It was now that the fovereign people, entering on their reign, firft took the famous
plundering motto : " *La guerre aux cha-
teaux et la paix aux chaumiéres ;*" that is,
*War to the gentlemen's houfes, and peace to the
cottage*; or, in other words, *war to all thofe
who have any thing to lofe.* This motto is
extremely comprehenfive; it includes the
whole doctrine of equality. It was not a
vain declaration in France; but was put
in practice with that patriotic zeal which

has marked the whole courfe of the revolution. To be rich, or of a good family, became a crime, which was often expiated by the lofs of life. Men took as much pains to be thought obfcure vagabonds, as they had formerly done to be thought wealthy and of honeft defcent; and, what diftinguifhes the French revolution from all others in the world, to have a ragged pair of breeches, or to be totally in want of that fo neceffary article of drefs, was efteemed the fureft mark of pure patriotifm, and was the greateft recommendation to public favour.

But the National Affembly, though heartily feconded by myriads of ragged populace, knew, however, that they could not long depend upon fuch a promifcuous fupport. The citizens were, therefore, to be foldiers at the fame time, and placed under the command of the creatures of the Affembly. To this end the territory of the nation underwent a new divifion, on the levelling plan. The provinces of France were melted down into a rude undigefted mafs of departments, diftricts, and municipalities. All the old magiftrates were replaced by the vileft wretches that could be found. There were forty four thoufand municipalities, each of thefe had feveral municipal officers, and each of thefe latter his troop of revolutionary myrmidons. There could not be lefs than *three millions* of men in arms, ready to burn, cut and flay at a moment's warning. Nothing was to be feen or heard but the patrolling of thefe fons of equality. The Affembly pretended to hold out the olive branch, while they were forming the nation into a camp. The peaceable man trembled for his life. One muft have been an eye witnefs of the change produced by thefe meafures, to have the leaft idea of it. All was fufpicion and dread. The bell that had never rung but to call the peaceful villagers to the altar, was converted to a fignal of approaching danger, and the tree, beneath which they formerly danced, became an alarm poft. The ragged greafy magiftrates, with their municipal troops at their heels, were for ever prowling about for their prey, the property of others. Thefe little platoons of cut-throats ranged the country round, crying havock, burning and laying wafte wherever they came. They had not yet begun to murder frequently, but it was little confequence to a man whether his brains were blowed out or not, after having feen himfelf and family reduced, in the fpace of a few hours, from affluence to beggary. A band of thefe enlightened ruffians went to the *chateau*, or country

houſe of a gentleman in Provence, and demanded that his perſon ſhould be delivered
into their hands. The ſervants defended
the houſe for ſome time, but in vain; they
advanced to the front door, when the lady
of the houſe appeared with a child in her
arms, and endeavoured to pacify them, ſay-
ing that her huſband was gone out at the
back door. The ruffians inſtantly ſet fire
to the houſe. When the lady perceived
this, ſhe confeſſed that her huſband was hidden in one of the garrets. The houſe was
now on fire; ſhe left her child, and ruſhed
through the flames to call her huſband from
his retreat, but ſhe was ſtifled in the paſſage,
and burnt to death, and her huſband ſhared
in her fate, leaving a helpleſs infant to the
mercy of the murderers of its father and mother.—A hundred volumes like this could
not contain the horrors that theſe revolutionary robbers committed in the name of
liberty and equality.

Let this, Americans, be a leſſon to you,
throw from you the doctrine of *equality*, as
you would the poiſoned chalice. Where-
ever this deteſtable principle gains ground
to any extent, ruin muſt inevitable enſue.
Would you ſtifle the noble flame of emula-
tion, and encourage ignorance and idleneſs?
Would you inculcate defiance of the laws?
Would you teach ſervants to be diſobedient

to their mafters, and children to their parents? Would you fow the feeds of envy, hatred, robbery, and murder? Would you break all the bands of fociety afunder, and turn a civilized people into a horde of favages? This is all done by the comprehenfive word equality.—But they tell us we are not to take it in the unqualified fenfe. In what fenfe are we to take it then? Either it means fomething more than liberty, or it means nothing at all. The mifconftruction of the word liberty has done mifchief enough in the world; to add to it a word of a ftill more dangerous extent, was to kindle a flame that never can be extinguifhed but by the total debafement, if not deftruction of the fociety, who are filly or wicked enough to adopt its ufe. We are told, that every government receives with its exiftence the latent difeafe that is one day to accomplifh its death; but the government that is attacked with this political apoplexy is annihilated in the twinkling of an eye.

The civil diforganization of the ftate was but the forerunner of thofe curfes which the Affembly had in ftore for their devoted country. They plainly perceived, that they never fhould be able to brutify the people to their wifhes, without removing the formidable barriers of religion and morality.

Their heads were turned, but it was neecf-
fary to corrupt their hearts.

Befides this, the leaders in the Affembly
were profeffed *modern philofophers*; that is to
fay, atheifts or deifts. Camus and Condorcet openly taught atheifm, and Ceruti
'faid with his laft breath, " *the only regret I*
" *have in quitting the world, is, that I leave a*
" *religion on earth.*" Thefe words, the blafphemy of an expiring demon, were applauded by the affembled legiflators. It was not
to be wondered at, that the vanity of fuch
men fhould be flattered in the hope of chang-
ing the *moft chriftian* country into the *moft
infidel* upon the face of the earth; for, there
is a fort of fanaticifm in irreligion, that leads
the profligate atheift to feek for profelytes
with a zeal that would do honour to a good
caufe, but which employed in a bad one be-
comes the fcourge of fociety.

The zeal of thefe philofophers for extirpat-
ing the truth was as great at leaft as that fhown
by the primitive chriftians for its propaga-
tion. But they proceeded in a very different
manner. At firft fome circumfpection was neceffary. The more effectually to deftroy the
chriftian religion altogether, they began by
fapping the foundations of the catholic faith,
the only one that the people had been taught
to revere. They formed a fchifm with the

church of Rome, well knowing that the
opinions of the vulgar, once fet afloat, were
as likely to fix on atheifm as on any other
fyftem ; and more fo, as being lefs oppofed
to their levelling principles than the rigid
though fimple morality of the gofpel. A
religion that teaches obedience to the higher
powers, inculcates humility and peace,
ftrictly forbids robbery and murder, and, in
fhort, enjoins on men to do as they would
be done unto, could by no means fuit the
armed ruffians, who were to accomplifh the
views of the French Affembly.

The prefs, which was made free for the
worft of purpofes, lent moft powerful aid to
thefe deftructive reformers. While the catholic religion was ridiculed and abufed, no
other chriftian fyftem was propofed in its
ftead ; on the contrary, the profligate
wretches who conducted the public prints,
among whom were Mirabeau, Marat, Condorcet and Hebert, filled one half of their
impious fheets with whatever could be
thought of to degrade all religion in general. The minifters of divine worfhip, of
every fect and denomination, were reprefented as cheats, and as the avowed enemies
of the fublime and fentimental fomething,
which the Affembly had in ftore for the re-
generation of the world.

Moſt of my readers muſt have heard of the magnificent church at St. Genviève, at Paris. It was one of the moſt noble ſtructures that the world had ever ſeen, and had beſides the honour of being conſecrated to the worſhip of Chriſt. This edifice the blaſphemers, ſeized on as a receptacle for the remains of their " *great men.*" From a chriſtian church, they changed it into a pagan temple, and gave it the name of *Pantheon.* Condorcet, pre-eminent in infamy, propoſed the decree, by which the name of God and that of St. Genviève were ordered to be effaced from the frontiſpiece.

To this *Pantheon* the aſhes of Voltaire were firſt tranſported, and the Aſſembly ſpent no leſs than three days in determining whether thoſe of *Rouſſeau* ſhould not accompany them. This diſtinction, paid to two of the moſt celebrated deiſts of the age, was a full declaration of the principles as well as the intentions of the majority of the Aſſembly.

Thoſe who have not had the patience to wade through the lies and blaſphemies of Voltaire, know his principles from report. *Rouſſeau* is not ſo well known; and, as he was, and ſtill continues to be, the great oracle of the revolutioniſts, I am perſuaded a page or two on his character, and that of his works, will not be loſt here; particularly as I have heard both mentioned with Applaufe in this country, by perfons apparently of the beft intentions.

The philofopher Rouffeau, the pagod of the regenerated French, was born at Geneva; and, at a proper age, bound an apprentice to an artift. During an apprenticefhip he frequently robbed his mafter as well as other perfons. Before his time was expired he decamped, fled into the dominions of the king of Sardinia, where he changed the prefbyterian for the catholic religion. This beginning feemed to promife fair for what followed. By an unexpected turn of fortune he became a footman, in which capacity he did not forget his old habit of ftealing. He is detected with the ftolen goods; fwears they were given him by a maid fervant of the houfe; the girl is confronted with him, fhe denies the fact, and weeping preffes him to confefs the truth; but the young philofopher ftill perfifts in the lie, and the poor girl is driven from her place in difgrace.—Tired of being a fervingman, he went to throw himfelf on the protection of a lady, whom he had feen once before, and who he protefts was the moft *virtuous* creature of her fex. This lady had fo great a regard of him, that he called him her *little darling*, and he called her *mama*. *Mama* had a footman, who ferved her be-

fides, in another capacity very much re-
lembling that of a hufband; but fhe had a
moft tender affection for her adopted fon
Rouffeau, and, as fhe feared he was forming
connections with a certain lady that might
fpoil his morals, fhe herfelf, out of pure virtue, took him—to bed with her!—This virtuous effort to preferve the purity of Rouffeau's heart, had a dreadful effect on the
head of the poor footman, and fo he poifon-
ed himfelf—Rouffeau fell fick, and *mama* was
obliged to part with *little darling*, while he
performed a journey to the fouth of France,
for the recovery of his health. On the road
he dines with a gentleman, and lies with his
wife. As he was returning back, he debat-
ed with himfelf whether he fhould pay this
lady a fecond vifit or not; but, fearing he
might be tempted to feduce her daughter
alfo, *virtue* got the better, and determined
the *little darling* to fly home into the arms
of his *mama*; but, alas! thofe arms were
filled with another. *Mama's* virtue had
prompted her to take a fubftitute, whom fhe
liked too well to part with, and our philofopher was obliged to fhift for himfelf. I
fhould have told the reader, that the *little*
darling, while he refided with his *mama*,
went to make a tour with a young mufician.
Their friendfhip was warm, like that of moft
young men, and they were, befides, enjoin-

ed to take particular care of each other during their travels. They travelled on for
fome time, agreed perfectly well, and vow-
ed an everlafting friendfhip for each other.
But, the mufician, being one day taken in a
fit, fell down in the ftreet, which furnifhed
the faithful Roufieau with an opportunity
of flipping off with fome of his things, and
leaving him to the mercy of the people, in
a town where he was a total ftranger.

We feldom meet with fo much villainy in
a youth. His manhood was worthy of it.
He turned apoftate a fecond time, was
driven from within the walls of his native
city of Geneva, as an incendiary, and an
apoftle of anarchy and infidelity; nor did
he forget how to thieve.—At laft the philofopher marries; but like a philofopher;
that is, without going to church. He has
a family of children, and, like a kind philofophical father, for fear they fhould want
after his death, he fends them to the *poor-
houfe* during his lifetime!—To conclude,
the philofopher dies, and leaves the philo-
fopherefs, his wife, to the protection of a
friend; fhe marries a footman, and gets
turned out into the ftreet.

This is a brief fketch of the life of Jean
Jacques Rouffeau, the oracle of the regenerated French, a thief, a whoremafter, an
adulterer, a treacherous friend, an unnatu-

ral father, and twice an apoſtate.—There wants only about a hundred murders to make him equal to the immortal Marat, whom we have ſeen compared to Jeſus Chriſt. This vile wretch has the impudence to ſay, in the work that contains a confeſſion of theſe his crimes, that no man can come to the throne of God, and ſay, *I am a better man than Rouſſeau.*

His writings, though they have very great literary merit, contain ſuch principles as might be expected from ſuch a man. He has exhauſted all the powers of reaſoning and all the charms of eloquence in the cauſe of anarchy and irreligion. And his writings are ſo much the more dangerous, as he winds himſelf into favour with the unwary, by an eternal cant about *virtue* and *liberty.* He ſeems to have aſſumed the maſk of virtue for no other purpoſe than that of propagating with more certain ſucceſs the blackeſt and moſt incorrigible vice *.

* Two philoſophers can ſeldom agree more than two perſons of any other profeſſion; ſo it happened with *Voltaire* and *Rouſſeau.* The humorous prophetic ſatire of the former, occaſioned by the publication of *Rouſ-ſeau's* romance, the *New Eloiſa,* is ſo well worthy of a place here, that I cannot deny myſelf the pleaſure of tranſlating an extract or two from it.

" In thoſe days there will appear in France a wonderful man. He will ſay unto the people, behold! I am poſſeſſed by the demon of enthuſiaſm; I have re-

This was the man and the writer that the conftituent Affembly held up to the imitation and even adoration of the poor deluded French people. The afhes of this thieving philofopher coft the nation almoft two thouſand guineas in debates.

Thoſe who know, what power novelty has on the French; with what enthufiaſm, or rather fury, they adopt whatever is in

ceived from heaven the gift of paradoxical inconfiftency; and the light-heeled multitude will dance after him and many will adore him. And he will fay, you are all raſcals and proftitutes, and I deteft rafcals and proftitutes, and I come to live amongft you. And he will add, the men and women are all virtuous in the republic of Geneva, where I was born, and I love virtuous men and women, and I will not live in the country where I was born.—He will proteft that the play-houfe is a fchool of proftitution and corruption, and he will write operas and plays.—He will advife mankind to go ſtark-naked, and he will wear laced cloths, when given unto him.—He will fwear that romances corrupt the morals of all who read them, and he will compofe a romance; and in this romance will be ſeen vice in deeds and virtue in words, and the lovers will be mad with love and with philofophy; and this romance will teach how to feduce a young girl philofophically; and the difciple will lofe all fhame and modefty: and fhe will practife foolifhnefs, and raife maxims and paradoxes with her mafter; and fhe will kifs firft, and afk him to lie with her, and he will actually lie with her, and fhe will become round and pregnant with metaphyfics. And this they will call philofophy and virtue, and they will talk about philofophy and virtue, till no foul on earth will know what philofophy and virtue is."

vogue, may guess at the effect that this phi-losophical canonization of Rousseau pro-duced. Every thing was *a la Rousseau*; his works were hawked about, mouthed in the National Assembly (often by those who un-derstood them not) recommended in all the prints, and spouted at the sans-culotte clubs. His old boorish sayings became the livelieft traits of wit, all his manners were imitated, to be crusty and ill-bred was like Jean Jacques, and, what was particularly offen-five to every juft mind, his loathsome down-looking portrait, that portrait which seems to be the chosen seat of guilt, was seen at every corner, and in every hand.

Having thus prepared the public mind, the Assembly made a bold attack on the church. They discovered, by the light of philosophy, that France contained too many churches, and, of course, too many paftors. Great part of them were therefore to be suppressed, and to make the innovation go down with the people, all tithes were to be abolished. The measure succeeded; but what did the people gain by the aboli-tion of the tithes? not a farthing; for, a tax of twenty *per cent.* was immediately laid on the lands in consequence of it. The cheat was not perceived till it was too late.

P

But, the abolition of the thithes, the only motive of which was to debafe the clergy in the opinions of the people, was but a trifle to what was to follow. The religious orders, that is to fay, the communities of monks and nuns, poffeffed immenfe landed eftates, and thefe the honeft Affembly had marked for their own. As a pretext for the feizure they firft decreed, that the wealth of the religious orders *belonged to the nation,* to that indefinite being, that exifts every where and no where, and that has devoured all, without receiving any thing.

As this act of feizing the eftates of the regular clergy, was one of thofe that gave a decifive blow to property as well as religion in France, and one that has received the greateft applaufes in this country, I fhall enter a little at length into the flagrant injuftice of it. Nor is the fubject-inapplicable to ourfelves ; for, though there are no religious orders in America, there are many people of property, and it is of a violation of property that I here charge the Affembly.

How the eftates of the religious orders became the property of a certain fomebody called the nation, in 1791, is to me wholly inconceiveable ; feeing that there never was a time, when they belonged to that fociety of men, now called the French. Great

part of the monafteries had been founded
five, fix, feven hundred years, and fome
above a thoufand years before the moft
worthlefs of the French took it into their
heads to be fo many fovereigns. The
founders were men of pious and auftere
lives, who, wifhing to retire from the
world, obtained grants of uncultivated land,
generally in fome barren and folitary fpot.
There they formed little miferable fettle-
ments, which, by their frugality and labour, in time became rich meadows, farms
and vineyards. A French hiftorian, fpeaking of St. Etienne, fays : " In 1058, he
" retired to Citeaux, then a vaft foreft, in-
" habited only by wild beafts. Here, with
" the help of his followers, he built a mo-
" naftery of the wood of the foreft; but,
" at firft, it was no more than a group of
" fhabby huts. Every thing bore the
" marks of extreme poverty : the crofs was
" of wood, the cenfers of copper, and the
" candlefticks of iron. All the ornaments
" were of coarfe woollen or linen. La-
" bour was the only means of fubfiftence
" with the monks of Citeaux. For many
" years bread was their only food, and they
" were often reduced to a fcarcity of even
" that."

In time this foreft became a cultivated
and flourifhing eftate, and the fucceffors of

the firſt proprietors were not only at their
eaſe, but even rich. The monaſtery, which
was at firſt but a clump of ill-ſhaped huts,
built with the limbs of trees, bark and turf,
was become a magnificent pile. ·The church
was beautiful beyond deſcription. Inſtead
of wood and copper and iron, the ſymbols
of religion and the ſacred vaſes were now of
gold, ſilver and precious ſtones. This
abbey, at the time of the ſeizure by the
Conſtituent Aſſembly, had an annual reve-
nue of 120,000 French livres, or, about
6000 pounds ſterling.

Now, I aſk any honeſt man, was this
the property of the French nation, or not?
By what rule of right, by what principle of
law or juſtice, could this eſtate belong to
any other than the *lawful* ſucceſſors of the
firſt proprietors; that is to ſay, the poſſeſ-
ſors at the epoch of the ſeizure? No title
ever framed by man could be ſo good as
theirs. The community at Citeaux had
never ceaſed to exiſt, nor for a ſingle moment
ceaſed to keep poſſeſſion of their Abbey and
its dependencies. They had firſt obtained
a lawful grant of the land, had cleared,
cultivated, and enriched it; and had enjoyed an uninterrupted poſſeſſion during the
ſpace of ſeven hundred and thirty two years?
but, at the end of the *enlightened* eighteenth
century, the *Age of Reaſon,* up ſtarts a horde

of lazy worthlefs ruffians, calling themfelves the nation, and lay claim to their
eftates !

Bulteau, in fpeaking of St. Benedict,
fays : " The bodily labour ordered by this
" wife founder, was a fource of peace and
" tranquility to the firft monks, and of
" opulence to their fucceffors. The mo-
" nafteries were long an afylum to thofe
" chriftians, who fled from the oppreflions
" of the Goths and Vandals. The little
" learning that remained in the barbarous
" and dark ages was preferved in the
" cloifters. It is to them we owe all the
" moft precious remains of antiquity, as
" well as many modern inventions."—Indeed, under the great difpofer of all events,
it is to them we owe that we are chriftians ;
that we poffefs the word of God, our guide
to eternal life. They not only preferved this
ineftimable volume, but fpread it in every
country in the world. Without their agen-
cy, our anceftors might have continued
pagans ; nay, we ourfelves, perhaps, might
now have been facrificing our children in
the hollow of a Wicker-Idol.—Every man
of any reading knows, that the monafteries
have continued to enrich the world with
learned and ufeful productions. Some of
the writings that do the greateft honour to

the French nation, and to the human mind, have iſſued from the cloiſter. And yet, we have ſeen theſe men robbed of their eſtates, ſtripped of even their furniture and their veſtments, driven from beneath their roofs, hunted like wild beaſts, and, what I am aſhamed to ſay, many of us have had the folly, or rather baſeneſs, to applaud their unprincipled and blood-thirſty purſuers *.

* I cannot help obſerving here, that theſe unjuſt and inhuman applauders have not always been confined to the mob. An " *Oration* on the *Progreſs of* " *Reaſon*," delivered at a Public Commencement in the Univerſity of Cambridge, Maſſachuſetts, on the 18th of July, 1792, contains a philippic againſt the injured French Monarch and Clergy, the moſt illiberal that ever diſgraced the lips of a petulant ſelf-ſufficient pedant. The *Orator* diſcovers but little knowledge of any branch of his ſubject, and more particularly of the character of Louis XVI. of that of the French Clergy, and of the nature of the old government; againſt all which he runs on in a ſtrain of invective, more reſembling the brutal abuſiveneſs of Calvin, than any thing we ought to expect to hear from the chair of a ſeminary, at the cloſe of the " *enlightened* eighteenth century."— Like many others, this *Orator* looked upon the French Revolution as happily terminated; as the dawn of univerſal peace, liberty, and virtue; he has ſince had time to ſee his error, to ſee the effects of his " Progreſs of " Reaſon," ſome of which I have related in the former part of this volume; if he be candid, therefore, he will publicly retract this error. If he ſhould not do this, I ſhall take the liberty, one of theſe days, of convincing him that he has erred.

We are told that the monks were become too rich. Indeed this was their great offence in the eyes of an Affembly, whofe motto was : " War to the rich and peace " to the cottager." But we have feen that the foundation of thefe riches was laid by the labour of their predeceffors, and · we may obferve that they were augmented, not by oppreffion, as has been falfely afferted, but by a prudent management of their eftates. Thofe communities that cultivated their own lands, were noted for the excellent manner of their cultivation, and for the fuperior quality of their produce ; and thofe that rented out their farms let them at a low rate, fo as to enable the farmer to enrich the land at the fame time that he enriched himfelf. It was by fuch means that their eftates became the moft valuable in the country, a circumftance that poor fhallow-headed Paine has brought againft them as a heinous offence. They were gentle humane mafters and landlords : a man looked upon his fortune as made, when he became the tenant of a religious order.

And, how were thefe riches fpent ? Not in horfes and coaches ; people fhut up in a cloifter had no ufe for thefe. Not in balls and plays ; for there they could never appear. Not in rich attire and coftly repafts ; for the greateft part of them were clothed

worfe than common beggars, and were forbidden the ufe of meat, and even of wine,
the common drink of their country. Their
riches did not go to aggrandize their families; becaufe, as no individual could poffefs any thing, fo he could bequeath or dif-
pofe of nothing. Who, then, profited
from thefe riches?—Go afk the poor, who
were happy in the neighbourhood of their
convents. Go afk the aged, the infirm, the
widow and the orphan. And, afk them, too,
what aid and confolation they have received
from the thieving philofophers of the Revolution.

This charge of being *too rich*, is the moft
abfurd as well as the moft vile that could
poffibly be invented. Do we fay to a man,
who has acquired an immenfe fortune by the
labour of his father, or by any other means;
you are *too rich*, and therefore your property
belongs to the nation?—There is a community at Bethlehem, very much refembling
thofe we have here been fpeaking of. What
fhould we think of a fcoundrel legiflator,
who fhould propofe to ftrip thefe people of
their property, and turn them out to beg
their bread, merely becaufe the value of
their lands is increafed? Such was he who
firft propofed the feizure of the church lands
in France.

Some of the convents in France had been founded by lay perfons, upon fuch and fuch conditions; and, in cafe of failure on the part of the community, the property was to revert to the heirs of the donor. Foundations of this kind were exactly re-fembling thofe we frequently fee among us, of hofpitals, feminaries, &c. and the deeds were ftill in exiftence at the time of the feizure; but an Affembly that paid no re-fpect to a right of prefcription, founded on a thoufand years of uninterrupted poffeffion, could not be expected to pay attention to the contents of a bit of old parchment.

We ought not to be aftonifhed at hear-ing the author of *The Age of Reafon* attempt to juftify this act of impudent fraud; but let us fee how his doctrine would fuit, if applied to ourfelves: for this is the only way to determine on its merits. Suppofe (which God forbid!) the principles of the French Revolution fhould be adopted by our Legif-lature, and they fhould declare all the meet-ing-houfes, feminaries, hofpitals, &c. toge-ther with the eftates which have been left for their fupport, *the property of the nation*, how fhould we receive this? Suppofe an army of cut-throats fhould be fent to the Friends Meeting-houfe and thruft them out with the points of their bayonets; fuppofe another fhould go to the epifcopal church, drive the congregation from the altar, strip the minister of his caffock, feize on the facramental cup, and turn the church into a ftable; I afk how fhould we like this?—But, we are told, there is a vaft difference; that the monks were fuperftitious drones, ufelefs to fociety.—Ah! let us beware. Let us take care not to condemn, becaufe we are proteftants, a religion that differs from our own in form only; a religion that has yet more votaries than any other chriftian profeffion can boaft of. And, as to the religious orders being ufelefs to fociety, we have no proofs of this, but ftrong prefumptive ones of the contrary; for, we know, that France was great and happy, that it had been increafing in extent, wealth and population, fince the exiftence of thofe communities. However, I can by no means take upon me to prove the public utility of the monaftic life; nor is it neceffary; for, if no man is to poffefs property, unlefs he can prove his utility to fociety, I am afraid that few of us would be fecure. How many hundreds of proprietors do we fee, who are much *worfe* than ufelefs to fociety! Surely the public is as much benefited by a man who fpends his life in a convent, as by one who fpends it in a tavern, at a billiard-table, or in a playhoufe. Thoufands and thoufands there are who never worked a ftroke, nor ſtudied a ſingle hour; vegetating mortals, who ſeem to live only to eat and drink, and be carried about. Yet we have never thought of ſeizing their eſtates. No; utility or inutility has nothing to do with the matter; the queſtion before us is a ſimple queſtion of right. Whether monks were neceſſary or uſeful in France, or not, we know there were ſuch people, and that they poſſeſſed property legally acquired; and every honeſt man, capable of diſtinguiſhing between right and wrong, will hold in abhorrence the Aſſembly that dared to rob them of it.

When we hear of ſuch crying acts of injuſtice as this, we are naturally led to enquire who were the firſt promoters of them. The reader will be aſtoniſhed to hear, that the decree for this national robbery was firſt propoſed by a biſhop. Of a hundred and thirty eight French biſhops, there were only *four* to be found, who would give their approbation to this deed, and one of theſe four was he who propoſed the decree. The Abbé Barruel ſpeaks of him in the following terms: " The Aſſembly thought it high
" time to conſummate their deſigns upon the
" church, by ſeizing what ſtill remained of
" its poſſeſſions. This meaſure was ſo evi-
" dently contrary to every principle of juſ-
" tice and common honeſty, that it was not

" eafy to find a man fo totally loft to every
" fentiment of humanity as to bring it for-
" ward. This fecond Judas was at laft
" found in the college of the apoftles. This
" was *Taillerand Perigord*, bifhop of Au-
" tun.—This Perigord poffeffed all the bafe-
" nefs, all the vices of a Jew."—*See hift. of
the French clergy, page 15.*

To obtain the fanction of the people to
this act, they were told, that the wealth of
the church would not only pay off the national debt, but render taxes in future un-
neceffary. No deception was ever fo bare-
faced as this; but even this was not wanted ; for the people themfelves had already
begun to tafte the fweets of plunder. Avarice tempted the trading part of the nation
to approve of the meafure. At the time
of paffing the decree they were feen among
the firft to applaud it. They faw an eafy
means of obtaining thofe fine rich eftates,
the poffeffion of which they had, perhaps, .
long coveted. In vain were they told, that
the purchafer would partake in the infamy
of the robbery; that, if the title of the
communities could not render property
fecure, that fame property could never be
fecure under any title the plunderers could
give. In vain were they told, that in fanctioning the feizure of the wealth of others,
they were fanctioning the feizure of their

own, whenever that all-devouring monfter, the fovereign people, fhould call on them for it. In vain were they told all this: they purchafed: they faw with pleafure the plundered clergy driven from their dwellings; but fcarcely had they taken poffeffion of their ill-gotten wealth, when not only that, but the remains of their other property were wrenched from them. Since that we have feen decree upon decree launched forth againft the rich: their account books have been fubmitted to public examination: they have been obliged to give drafts for the funds they poffeffed even in foreign countries; all their letters have been intercepted and read. How many hundreds of them have we feen led to the fcaffold, merely becaufe they were proprietors of what their fovereign ftood in need of! thefe were acts of unexampled tyranny; but, as they refpected the perfons who applauded the feizure of the eftates of the church, they were perfectly juft. Several of thefe avaricious purchafers have been murdered within the walls of thofe buildings, whence they had affifted to drive the lawful proprietors: this was juft: it was the meafure they had meted to others. They fhared the fate of the injured clergy, without fharing the pity which that fate excited. When dragged

Q

forth to flaughter in their turn, they were left without even the right of complaining : the laft ftab of the affaffin was accompanied with the cutting reflection, that it was juft.

I have dwelt the longer on this fubject, as it is, perhaps, the moft ftriking and moft awful example of the confequences of a violation of property, that the world ever faw. Let it ferve to warn all thofe who wifh to raife their fortunes on the ruin of others, that fooner or later, their own turn muft come. From this act of the Conftituent Affembly we may date the violation, in France, of every right that men ought to hold dear. Hence the feizure of all gold and filver as the property of the nation : hence the law preventing the fon to claim the wealth of his father : hence the abominable tyranny of requifitions ; and hence thoufands and thoufands of the murders, that have difgraced unhappy France.

Since the feizure of the church eftates, there has not, in fact, been any fuch thing as private property in France ; for, though the Conftituent Affembly did not pafs a decree of this impot, they knew perfectly well how to pafs decrees and eftablifh regulations amounting to the fame thing. Some of their enormous contributions on the rich, were called *patriotic gifts* ; but he who refufed to pay the *gift* inferted in the lift, knew

,he had but a few hours to live. The money and jewels, depofited at the bar of the Affembly and on the altar of the country, amounted to immenfe fums. Thefe were held out as a proof of a general approbation of their meafures; but had the Affembly been candid, they would have confeffed, that thefe offerings were the pure effect of fear, of a panic that had feized all the proprietors in the nation, and that each giver's hatred to their caufe might be meafured by the fum he depofited. It was not a grateful free-will offering, but a facrifice, that the trembling wretch came to offer at the fhrine of tyranny, in order to fave his houfe from the flames, or his own head, or that of fome dear relation or parent from the fcaffold. Could a man, reduced to acts like this, be faid to *poffefs* any thing?

The fucceffors of the Conftituent Affembly laid afide the mafk, as no longer neceffary. On the 13th of March, 1794, all the Merchants of Bourdeaux (known for one of the moft infamoufly patriotic towns in the kingdon) were arrefted in one day, and condemned, in prefence of the guillotine, to a fine of *one hundred millions* of French livres, upwards of *four millions fterling*. On the 18th of April, the rich Banker, La Borde, after having *purchafed his life eight times*, was guillotined, and the remainder of his riches confiscated. On the 10th of May, twenty-seven rich Farmers-General were executed, because they had massed riches under the monarchy. Finally, on the 27th of June, all property, of whatever description, was decreed *to belong to the nation*, and was put in a state of requisition accordingly, as the *persons* of the whole of the inhabitants had been before.

The milk-and-water admirers of the Constituent Assembly pretend to be shocked at these measures; but, what are these measures more than an improvement on those of that Assembly? The progress was not only natural, but even necessary to the support of the revolution. Had there been still church-estates to seize, and monks to murder, it is probable, that the tyrants, who have succeeded the Constituent Assembly, would not have surpassed their predecessors; but, that source being exhausted, they were obliged to find out others, or return to order and obedience. And, I should be glad to know, if the property of one individual, or one society, was become the property of the sovereign people by virtue of a decree of one Assembly, why the same claim should not be made to the property of other individuals, or other societies. Nor can I believe, whatever Atheists and

Deifts may fay to the contrary, that it was any more unjuft to guillotine Bankers and Merchants, or even *members of the Conftitu- ent Affembly*, than to guillotine or maffacre poor, defencelefs, friendlefs Priefts. There is fuch an intimate connection between the fecurity of property, and that of the perfon to whom that property belongs, that one can never be faid to be fafe, while the other is in danger. Tyrant princes, tyrant affem- blies, or tyrant mobs, when once they are fuffered to take away with impunity the property of the innocent man, will feel lit- tle fcruple at taking away his life alfo. Robbery and murder are the natural auxi- liaries of each other, and, with a people rendered ferocious and hardened by an in- fidel fyftem that removes all fear of an here- after, they muft for ever be infeparable.

Before the decree was paffed for the af- fumption of the eftates of the regular clergy, every calumny that falfhood could invent, and every vexation that Tyranny could en- force, were employed to debafe the whole body of the clergy and the religion they taught. Songs and caricatures were fung, or hawked about, by fhamelefs ftrumpets in the pay of the Affembly. In thefe not only the clerical functions and the lives of the clergy were ridiculed, but even the life of

Jefus Chrift and the Virgin Mary. The *Incarnation* of our Saviour became the fubject of a *farce*, in the fmutty language of Parifian fifh-women. Who were the characters in this farce, I leave the fhuddering reader to conceive.

A decree, in form of an *invitation* *, was iffued, for bringing the gold and filver from the churches to the mint. It was well known, that there were none of thefe metals in the churches, except the vafes, the crucifixes, and other fymbols, hitherto held facred. What an effect the coining up of thefe muft have on the minds of the giddy multitude, is not difficult to imagine. Many, however, even of the moft depraved, felt a momentary horror; but this horror the Affembly knew how to do away. Hundreds, I might fay thoufands, of abandoned fcriblers were employed to propagate the new principles. Their little filthy ditties were fpread through all the departments, *at the expence of the nation.* Some of thefe

* " Invitations from fuperiors," fays fome one, " favour ftrongly of commands." This was fo much the cafe in the prefent inftance, that the prieft who dared to difobey, was fure to expiate his difobedience with his life. The magiftrates often entered the church and feized the chalices on the altar, during the celebration of the mafs. Such are revolutionary *invitations.*

were catechifms in rhyme, in which the
Conftitution was fubftituted for God, the
Affembly for the faints, and both recommended to the adoration of the French patriots. The journal, or Letter, as it was
called, of *Pere du Chêne*, written by one
Hebert, and of which it is faid fifty thoufand copies were ftruck off daily, was fent
into the towns and villages by the carriers
of the decrees of the Affembly. This Hebert, whofe Strumpet has fince been adored
at Paris, as the Goddefs of *Reafon*, was a
profeffed atheift. His journal contained the
moft outrageous abufe of all that was refpectable and facred, interlarded with oaths
and execrations without number. I have
one now before me, which has for title:
" *Lettre du veritable Pere du Chêne, bougre-*
" *ment patriotic*," in Englifh : " Letter of
" the true Father du Chêne b—gerly pa-
" triotic ;" I would here infert an extract
from this letter ; but, I truft I fhall be believed, when I fay, the contents are fully
anfwerable to the title. Such were the
agents of Condorcet and his colleagues :
thus did they corrupt the morals of the people ; thus did they lead them from one degree of vice to another ; thus were they hardened up to rob and to murder ; and thus
did the boafted Conftituent Affembly lay

the foundation of all thofe horrors we have fince heard of.

The magiftrates in the different municipalities, chofen from the fcum of the nation, diftributed thefe infernal writings among the people in their precincts, and particularly among the young people. If, by chance, fome magiftrate was found, too fcrupulous to execute their will, means were foon invented to get rid of him. Some pretext or other was never wanting to excite the mob to put an end to him and his refiftance. Chatel, Mayor of St. Denys, was one of this defcription. The mob were told that this man was the caufe of the dearnefs of bread. They flew to his houfe, and obliged him to reduce the price according to their will; though it was well known, that he had not the power to reduce it at all unlefs at his own expence. The rabble were difperfing; but they had not fulfilled the bloody wifhes of the revolutionary agents, who had nothing lefs in view than the lowering of the price of bread. They were inftigated to return to the unfortunate magiftrate. Firft, they attempted to hang him; but, wearied with his refiftance, one of them took out his knife, and cut his head partly off, while feveral others pricked him with their bayonets. The unhappy victim was ftill alive after the back of his neck was cut afunder, and was heard to groan out : " *for heaven's fake kill me ! kill* " *me ! you make me fuffer too long !*"—The fanguinary villain, who had begun to cut his head off, now threw away his knife, and borrowed that of his comrade, with which he finifhed the work. When he found that his own knife was not fufficient, he faid, with a cool indifference : " *lend me your* " *knife, for mine is not worfe a curfe.*" That which was lent him was a little twopenny knife with a wooden handle.—During this time, other affaffins gave him feveral ftabs, with their knives, in the belly and ftomach ; one of them turned his knife flowly in the flank of the dying man, and faid to him, laughing : " *Does that enter well ? Don't* " *you find the day-light peep into you ?*"—He at laft expired, after the moft inconceivable torments. His body was dragged along the ftreets of St. Denys with his head tied to his feet.—A refolution of the town has fince declared him innocent of any offence whatever : he had given abundant affiftance to the poor the winter before : the diminu- tion he had juft made in the price of bread was at his own expence ; and this barbarous punifhment was his recompence. His wife went diftracted, and has ever fince been in a mad-houfe. His affaffins obtained pardon from the Aſſembly, a circumſtance much leſs ſurpriſing, than that they ſhould think it neceſſary to aſk it. *See du Cour's Memoire,* page 57.

Examples of this kind, and ſuch were wanting in very few parts of the country, could not fail to enſure an implicit obedience on the part of the magiſtrates.

The debaſement of religion was nearly completely by the public ſale of the ſuppreſſed churches and monaſteries. The groſſeſt indecency preſided at all theſe demoniac ſcenes. When the vile agent of the Aſſembly, hammer in hand, had exhauſted his auctioneer rhetoric, in recommending a church as an excellent barn, ſtable, or playhouſe, it was knocked down to the baſe and avaricious ſpeculator, while the hireling mob ſhouted applauſe. The church of St. Aldegonde at St. Omer's (I love to cite inſtances) the higheſt in that ancient town, and for hundreds of years the pride of its inhabitants, was ſold to a *Jew* of Dunkirk, for the pitiful ſum of 20,000 French livres in aſſignats, not more than 200 pounds ſterling, nor half the coſt of one of the pillars. This beautiful edifice, by the ſpire of which the town was known at a great diſtance, had been choſen for deſtruction, that the humiliation of religion might be the more ſtriking. It met with ſuch treatment as

might be expected from the hands of an infidel. Its lofty fpire was tumbled to the
earth in lefs than a month : the body of the
church was turned into a ropewalk, and the
Jew proprietor, to complete the degreda-
tion of Chriftianity, left a reprefentation of
the Lord's Supper uneffaced in the chancel.
What muft be the grief, what the indignation of the thinking and pious part of the inhabitants of St. Omer's, thus to fee their favourite church, the fanctuary of their God,
and the G d of their fathers, delivered, for
a bundle of depreciated paper-money, into
the hands of a defcendant of the murderers of
him, to whofe worfhip it was confecrated !

To give the reader a juft idea of the ribaldry
of the fcenes of brutal impiety, exhibited at
the pillages of the convents, is totally impoffible. A dozen or two of carts rattling along
with a commiffary at their head, followed by
an efcort of ragamuffins, decorated with a
bit of three-coloured ribbon, and armed
with hammers, axes, crow-bars and fpades,
generally formed the corps for fuch an expedition. Hardly were the doors opened,
when the vaults rang with their hammering
and their oaths. In a few hours the whole
was gutted. The decorations of the altar,
the prieft's veftments, ftatues, pictures,
books, manufcripts, the moft precious pieces
of antiquity, the productions of long and

laborious lives of study, were hauled away as so much rubbish. The paintings on the doors, walls, cielings, and other fixtures, were effaced or disfigured; the fury of the *enlightened* ruffians descended even to the graves of the deceased fathers.

At the expulsion of the nuns, the conduct of the revolutionists, was, if possible, still more swinish and cruel. While the gibing commissary pulled aside their veils to examine their faces, his blackguard attendants congratulated them on the *pleasures* they were going to enjoy in the world, and this in a language calculated to raise a blush on the cheek on a common street-walker. They seemed to enjoy their tears, and even to make some sacrifices to augment them. Had any one a piece of needlework which she wished to preserve, it was rent to pieces before her face. A singing bird that had the misfortune to have been the companion of the solitary hours of its mistress, was sure to be taken from her and killed. To these dejected and defenceless females, every insult and indignity was offered, not forgetting the last of which beastly libertines can be guilty.

In a country where the crucifix was sent to the mint, where churches were put up at auction; where the half-worn cassock, the surplice, and the veil, made part of the assortment of a dealer in old cloaths, and were expofed to public fale on the market-place; where the minifters of the gofpel were fcoffed at, reviled, and frequently murdered with as little ceremony as one would kill a dog; where the moft daring blafphemies were uttered and publifhed and fpread through the country, not only with the permiffion of its governors, but by their direction; in a country where all this was practifed, religion could not be of long duration. Religion, and even the Catholic religion, did, however, ftill fubfift in France, at leaft, in *form*. The Affembly had as yet paffed no pofitive decree for its abolition. They had robbed the church, had ftripped its altars, and degraded its minifters; but ftill the moft pious and active of thofe minifters were left in the exercife of their functions. The parochial clergy, though deprived of the tithes, had a ftipend allowed them. They yet remained with their parifhioners, many of whom, indeed nearly all the elderly and fober part of them, continued as firmly attached to their paftors, as at any former period.

Things were not fuffered to remain long in this ftate. The Conftituent Affembly well knew, that they and religion could never exift for any length of time in the fame country. The parochial clergy were

R

men of talents and induſtry. They generally decided all the little diſputes between their pariſhioners; to which amicable capacity, they often joined that of phyſician or ſurgeon; and theſe their beneficent ſervices were always rendered without fee or reward. Even the atheiſts and deiſts themſelves had repeatedly acknowledged their virtuous modeſty, and the great utility they were of to the community at large. Such a body of men, immoveably attached to the religion they taught, was truly formidable to the new tyrants. Religion had received a ſevere blow; but, if theſe men retained their cures, it might recover. Nay, what was ſtill more dreadful, the monarchy itſelf might recover along with it; and it is not difficult to conceive, how an idea like this muſt haunt the minds of the pupils of the ſavage and impious Diderot, who hoped to ſee "the laſt of kings ſtrangled with the "guts of the laſt of prieſts." In ſhort, the parochial clergy, were the only men on earth they had now to fear, and theſe they got rid of by a ſtratagem worthy of an Aſſembly, the leaders of which joined to the moſt hardened wickedneſs, the profoundeſt diſſimulation.

They laid aſide the *Rights of Man*, together with the famous conſtitution, from which they took the adjunct to their name,

and which we have fince feen burnt by the
hands of the common hangman (or rather
common guillotiner) in that very city of
Paris, where it had been iffued amidft the
applaufes and even adorations of the populace. They laid afide the difcuffion of this
inftrument of fhort-lived and ridiculous memory, to draw up another, which they
were pleafed to call, " the Civil Conftitution
of the Clergy." They were conftitution
mad, abfolutely frantic.

It might be fufficient to fay of this latter
conftitution, that it was juft as fubverfive of
religion as their other conftitution was of
every principle of government and found
policy. They knew it to be in direct oppofition to the very nature of the catholic
religion : yet they had the affurance to tell
the people, that it was not; they even went
fo far as to proteft, that they would live and
die in the religion of their forefathers, at the
very moment when they were taking the
fureft meafure in the world for deftroying
it. They were led to this hypocritical declaration from a fear that the body of the
people were not yet ripe for a total abolition
of religion, and, as we fhall fee in the fe-
quel, this fear was not entirely unfounded.
By perfuading the people, that nothing was
intended againft their faith, they had an
additional handle againft the clergy, by re-

prefenting them as unfriendly to their "Civil Conftitution," merely becaufe it was necef-fary to the fupport of the *Rights of Man.*

This inftrument did not, however, pafs into a law, without confiderable refiftance. There were yet fome honeft and virtuous men even among the members of the Con-ftituent Affembly. Thefe had remained with them, not to aid in overturning the government, and effecting the dreadful revolution that has fince rendered the coun-try a flaughter-houfe, but to oppofe the de-ftructive meafures of the philofophers, and, if poffible fave the finking ftate. At the head of thefe was the learned and eloquent Abbé Maury. He oppofed this "Civil Conftitution," with all the powers of rea-foning, and all the charms of eloquence: but it was cafting pearls before fwine. When was an atheift open to conviction. The decree paffed, and was foon after followed by another, obliging the clergy to fwear to obferve and maintain the "Civil Conftitu-tion." This oath they could not take without breaking that which they had taken at entering into the priefthood; and that the Affembly had every reafon to fuppofe they would not do. Whether they did or not, however, the end of their tyrants was anfwered: if they refufed, they were to be driven from their livings; if they complied, they mu?t be looked upon as apo?tates, and be de?erted by all tho?e who were ?till attached to them. In either ca?e the tottering remains of religion mu?t come to the ground. The clergy, and indeed the whole nation, and all Europe, ?aw the real obje?t of this inhuman and impious decree; but the A?-?embly, ?urrounded with their *enlightened* myrmidons, the Pari?ian mob, bid defiance to earth and heaven.

Generally ?peaking, the clergy were re-?olved not to take the oath. " Lo?e no " time," ?aid the Abbé Maury, " in the de-" livery of your challenge. By ?hedding " our blood you may ingratiate your?elves " with your con?tituents. Lo?e, then, not " a ?ingle moment. Your vi?tims are here; " they are ready. To their torments add " not that of ?u?pence. Why not vote at " once for our execution, glut your hatred, " and quench for a little your thir?t for " blood? Ha?ten, I ?ay, while the power " is in your hands; for remember, I now " foretel, *your reign will be of ?hort dura-* " *tion.*"

. This prophetic addre?s, which we have ?een ?o fully verified, ?erved only to inflame. Eight days only were given the clergy to determine on compliance or refu?al, during which no ?tratagem that ba?e and degene-

R 3

rate tyranny could devise, was left uneſſayed to intimidate them. This was ever their practice, when they had an important blow to ſtrike. Rochefoucauld, formerly a duke, declared, at the time the decree for the ſeizure of the monaſteries was under deliberation, that " *the lives of the biſhops and* " *prieſts, in the Aſſembly, depended upon the* " *paſſing of it*;" and, in order to ſilence all thoſe who oppoſed it, a liſt of their names was ſtuck up on the walls, with a promiſe of a reward of " twelve hundred livres *to* " *any patriot who would aſſaſſinate them.*" According to this laudable cuſtom, this inſtance of French liberty, when the day for taking the oath, or, as it was well-termed, " the for-ſwearing day" arrived, the Aſſembly took care to call in the aid of the fiſhwomen and mob. " *To the lamp-poſt with* " *the non-juring biſhops and prieſts!*" was echoed from the ſtreets and the galleries. The ruffians were prepared for murder, and were howling for their prey, like ſo many wolves round a ſheep-fold.

Let the reader imagine himſelf in the ſituation of one of theſe unfortunate clergymen: an oath of apoſtacy before him, and a halter behind his back, and then let him give me his opinion of the *rights of man.*

This did not intimidate the clergy, only thirty of whom could be prevailed on to submit, and thefe were already known to have abandoned their religion. When the oath was tendered to the bifhop of Agen, " Gentlemen," fays he, " I lament not the lofs of my fortune; but there is another " lofs which I fhould ever lament, the lofs " of your efteem and my faith. I could " not fail to lofe both, if I took the oath " now propofed to me." The old bifhop of Poitiers, fearing he might lofe fo fair an opportunity of bearing teftimony of his fin-cerity, advanced to the tribune, and call-ing on the prefident to command filence; " Gentlemen," faid he, " I am feventy " years o'd; I have been thirty years a bi-" fhop: I will never difgrace my gray hairs " by an oath of apoftacy." Upon this manly declaration of the reverend old pre-late, the clergy rofe from their feats, thank-ed him for his example, and told the Af-fembly he had expreffed their unanimous fentiments.

Not being a Roman Catholic, I hope I fhall be excufed, when I freely declare, that I much queftion, whether the minifters of any Proteftant communion, in a moment fo terrible, furrounded with affaffins, and without a fingle friend, would have fhown fuch a noble intrepidity. " They have

" loft their money," faid the profligate Mirabeau, on this occafion, " *but they have* " *faved their honour.*" * And, if this was

* Doctor Prieftley (Faft Sermon of 1794, page 46,) fays : " When I was myfelf in France, in 1774, I " faw fufficient reafon to believe, that *hardly any per-* " *fon of eminence,* in *church* or ftate, and efpecially in " the leaft degree eminent in *philofophy,* or literature, " was a believer in chriftianity ; and no perfon will " fuppofe that there has been any change in favour " of chriftianity *in the laft twenty years.*"—The Doctor will allow, I fuppofe, that bifhops are " per- " fons of *eminence* in the *church* ;" if he does, it will appear that he knew but very little of thofe of the French church, and that he formed a very rafh opinion (to fay the beft of it) concerning their be- lief in chriftianity ; for, of *one hundred and thirty- eight* bifhops, only four, namely, Taillerand, Brienne, Jarante, and Gobet, took the oath of apoftacy. But, he will fay ; I meant, " thofe *eminent* in *philofophy* " and literature." Ah ! eminent in *philofophy !* here he is right. No, no ; not one of the *philofophical divines* believed in chriftianity ; they looked upon Chrift, as the Unitarians do ; that is, as a fort of " teacher :" but, to the honour of the French bi- fhops, there were but four of thefe philofophers amongft them. As to the other *hundred and thirty,* if they have not given a proof of their belief, I fhould be glad to know from the Doctor, what proof he will pleafe to be fatisfied with.—Their refufal to take the oath could be dictated by nothing but their be- lief in chriftianity, and their determination not to dif- honour it. Had not this been the cafe, they would have taken the oaths, and preferved their fortunes. They were in a country where the mob do not, like thofe of Birmingham, content themfelves with the

the cafe, what had the Affembly done ? If, to *preserve honour*, it was neceffary to refufe an obedience to their decrees, what fort of decrees muft thofe be ? The Affembly were difconcerted by this firm refiftance on the part of the clergy ? they knew the clergy in general would never take the oath, but they did not imagine

execution of an *effigy*; they execute the perfon. Yet they remained at their poft : they did not *decamp in diiguife*. Even if they efcaped the knives of the cut-throats, they knew that poverty, beggary, a lingering exiftence, muft be the price of their refufal. They could not *bring an action againft the city of Paris :* no *damages* are granted by a jury in that country. They could not *preach and prate againft the government* with impunity; they could not *transfer their property, and emigrate in open day.* There are fuch things as national guards, municipalities, paffports, halters, daggers, knives, drowning-boats, and *the rights of man,* in France. We have fince feen feveral of thefe bifhops, or men " of eminence in the church," refufe, with the bloody poignard at their breafts, to take this oath. Would they have done this, had they been what Doctor Prieftley has reprefented them to be ? would they have done this, had they been atheifts or deifts ? nay, would they have done this, had they been *Unitarians ?* If we are to judge from the conduct of the Doctor, they would not.—I will not take upon me to fay, that the philofophical political divine meant to propagate an atrocious calumny by this fermon of his : I fhall only obferve, that the fermon was preached long after the French bifhops had given thefe undeniable proofs of their faith and fincerity.

that thofe amongft themfelves, would,
amidft the vociferations of their cannibals,
have the courage to give fuch a pofitive de-
nial. For a moment they felt abafhed;
but they were gone too far to think of re-
treating. The apoftate Abbé Gregoire,
whom we have fince feen amongft the organizers of a pagan feftival, was, on this
occafion chofen to convince the clergy, that
the oath might be taken, without any violation of their faith. After this, in order
to deprive the clergy of an opportunity of
defending their opinions in oppofition to
the oath, they were ordered to advance and
take it at once. This decree had no effect:
not a man advanced. Now the matter was
brought to a point: the decree for enforcing
the oath muft be repealed, or the clergy
muft be driven from their livings, and thofe
in the Affembly from their feats. It is
hardly neceffary to fay that the latter was
adopted: one tyrannical meafure is the natural and inevitable confequence of another.

A decree was now paffed for the expulfion of all the non-juring bifhops and priefts,
and for the choofing of others in their ftead.
From this day, it may be faid, there was
no fuch thing as an eftablifhed religion in
France. The axe had long been laid to the
root of the tree; it was ready to fall, and
this ftroke levelled it with the earth.

Had the difpute been about this or that
tenet, had the oath been impofed with an
intention of exchanging one religion for another, the cafe would have been different; the
expulfion might have taken place without
any very confiderable injury to the morals
of the people. But, the ftruggle was that
of religion againft irreligion, that of chriftianity againft atheifm.

It was (I hope it is fo no longer) the
opinion of Doctor Prieftley, and many other
philofophical divines, that *any change whatever* was preferable to the continuation of
the catholic religion in France. There is a
paffage in Moore's journal, which contains
fo complete an anfwer to every thing thefe
gentlemen have advanced on this fubject,
that I am furpifed, confidering the principles of the journalift and his companion
Lauderdale, that it ever found a place in
that volume.

The Doctor, being an Abbeville, met
with a proteftant clergyman, whom he congratulated on the deliverance of himfelf and
his brethren, from the vexation of Romifh
perfecution. The clergyman feemed to lament, that along with the fpirit of perfecution, that of religion daily diminifhed.
" Upon which," fays the Doctor, " I ob-
" ferved that, as nothing could be more
" oppofite to true religion than a fpirit of

" perfecution, the former, it was to be
" hoped, would return without the latter;
" but, in the mean time, the proteftants
" were happy in not only being tolerated in
" the exercife of their religion, but alfo on
" being rendered capable of enjoying every
" privilege and advantage which the catho-
" lics themfelves enjoy.

" We are not allowed thofe advantages,
" refumed the clergyman, from any regard
" they bear to our religion, but from a total
" indifference of their own.

" Whatever may be the cafe, replied I,
" the effeƈt is the fame with regard to you.

" No, faid he, the effeƈt might be bet-
" ter, not only with refpeƈt to us, but to
" all France : for the fpirit of perfecution
" might have difappeared, without an in-
" difference for all religion coming in its
" place : and in that cafe there would have
" been more probability of the true reli-
" gion gaining ground ; for it is eafier to
" draw men from an erroneous doƈtrine to
" a true one, than to imprefs the truths of
" religion on minds which defpife all reli-
" gion whatever.

" But, although you may not be able to
" make converts of them, I replied, ftill
" you may live happy among them, in the
" quiet poffeffion of your own religion and
" all your other advantages.

" I doubt it much, refumed he ; being
" perfuaded that, in a country where re-
" ligious fentiments are effaced from the
" minds of the bulk of the people, crimes
" of the deepeft guilt will prevail in fpite of ·
" all the reftraints of law."

How fully, alas ! has the opinion of this
good clergyman been confirmed ! here we
fee a man living upon the fpot, a Frenchman and a proteftant, lamenting the de-
cay of the catholic religion, and trembling
for the confequences. This man plainly
perceived the drift of the philofophical legiflators : he faw that the deftruction of
all religion was their object, while they
pretended to be correcting its abufes.
Very far was he from faying, with our
zealous reformers, that " any change was
" preferable to the continuation of popery,"
and yet, I think, we ought to allow him
to be as much interefted in a change, and
as good a judge of its conveniences and in-
conveniences, as perfons on this fide the
fea ; except, indeed, that he might not be
enlightened by the rays of modern philofophy.*.

---

* Some of the French proteftants, however, dif-
fered widely from this good man. The Calvinifts of
Nimes began maffacreing the Catnolics at an early period of the revolution, under the pretext that they

From this digreſſion we muſt return to the expulſed clergy. The pariſh prieſts generally followed the example of their biſhops, in refuſing to take the oath. Others were, of courſe, appointed to replace them. *Taillerand Perigord*, whom we have ſeen propoſing the aſſumption of the church eſtates, was now become a ſort of Pope to the modern church, and was buſily employed, laying *unholy hands* on the heads of the new biſhops. *Gobet*, one of the four bi-

---

were *ariſtocrats*. About ſix hundred perſons, of both ſexes and of all ages, were butchered in their houſes, in the ſtreets and public ſquares, before they could even ſuſpect their danger. Theſe monſters attacked the convent of the capuchins, forced it open, and purſued the venerable fathers to their dormitories and cells. Five of them were left weltering in their blood at the altar's foot. One of theſe, a very o'd man, craved five minutes while he committed his ſoul to God. The cool and deliberate villains granted his requeſt. The intended butcher held a piſtol in one hand, and a watch in the other, and, when the five minutes were expired, ſhot him through the head. *See Hiſt. of the French Clergy, page* 71. *French edition.*

This fact fully proves, that proteſtants can be as cruel as catholics. Let us not, then, imagine that we are ſecure from events of this kind, merely becauſe the catholic religion is not eſtabliſhed here. It was not a zeal for the Calviniſtical religion that led the proteſtants of Nimes to commit theſe acts of barbarity : their knives were pointed, not againſt catholics, as ſuch, but as *ariſtocrats*.

fhops who had forfworn themfelves, was re-
warded for his apoftacy by the bifhoprick
of Paris. Vagabond philofophical abbés,
who had never been able to obtain admittance into the priefthood under the old
government, were now not only accepted,
but fought after. To thefe were added the
fecular priefts and monks who had apofta-
tized. Even the wretches who had been expulfed from their cures, or orders, for irre-
gular or criminal conduct, were now called
in from Germany and the Low Countries.
What a fight muft it be, to thofe who yet
preferved fome refpect for their religion
and their country, to fee thefe ftrollers,
with their ftrumpets at their heels, returning to take on them the care of the morals
and fouls of a numerous people! after all,
the number of apoftates was infufficient: a
great many parifhes remained without any
prieft at all.

The inftallment of the new priefts was
commonly, not to fay always, attended
with tumult and violence. Many of their
predeceffors were knocked down, ftabbed, or
fhot, at their church doors, the day, or
day after, they had refufed to conform.
The prieft of the village of Spet-Saux, while
he was explaining to his parifhioners his rea-
fons for refufing to take the oath, received

a mufket ball in his breaft, and tumbled dead
from the pulpit into the aifle.

Where there was no refiftance but on
the part of the prieft, an affaffination put an
end to the ftruggle; but, in fome places, the
refiftance was more general. The parifhioners were divided; one part the
champions of the apoftate, and the other,
thofe of the old prieft. Church time was
the moment for deciding thefe difputes, and
the Church-yard the field of action.
Thefe affrays were often bloody; victory
fometimes leaned to the fide of juftice; but,
as the apoftate appeared in perfon at the
head of his troops, as he had the young people generally on his fide, and always the
mob and municipal officers, with their national guards, he feldom failed to keep the
field. Some of thefe wretches have been
feen conducted to the altar to the found of
drums and trumpets, at the very moment
when their partizans were murdering on
the outfide of the church.

The expelling of the parochial clergy
tried the real fentiments of the body of the
French people more than any one act of
their tyrants ever did, before or fince. Generally fpeaking, the trial was honourable
to them; for, if we except Paris, and fome
other places immediately under the influence of the revolutionary clubs, they wifhed

to retain their ancient paftors, and did not fcruple to declare that wifh, notwithftanding the vociferations of hundreds of mob in the pay of the Affembly; notwithftanding all thefe petty affemblies of fubaltern tyrants, called municipal officers, who came to order them to receive an apoftate, *in the name of the law*; notwithftanding thoufands of fpies and affaffins, ever ready to betray and murder them; in fpite of all thefe, whole parifhes flocked round their priefts, preffed them to continue, followed them to the fields, and left the apoftates to fay mafs to the bare walls. Many of the latter, though they continued to receive the revolutionary falary for upwards of two years, never could boaft of above three or four voluntary hearers.

Wherever this obftinate attachment to religion appeared, the Affembly knew how to make the refractory feel their authority. True tyrants, they fuffered no one to thwart their will with impunity. Property, honour, confcience, all muft yield to their fultanic decrees!

Condorcet, the atheift Condorcet, propofed flagellation; and this was pretty commonly inflicted on the women and children who affifted at the maffes of the non-juring clergy. The Abbé Barruel (page 79 of the

S 3

French edition) tells us, that three fifters of one of the Charity-houfes at Paris, expired under the rods of the affaffins. Ungrateful monfters ! the lives of thefe women had been totally devoted to the fervice of the fick, the lame and the blind. By their vow they were excluded from the pleafures of the world, without being excluded from its pains. They had made a voluntary furren-der of all they poffeffed, had affumed the garb, and fubmitted to the aufterities of the monaftic life, in order to devote themfelves to the mournful occupation of attending on the *poor* who laboured under infirmities. It was faid, they did this to fecure themfelves a place in heaven; and moft certainly they took the fureft way. I feel a reluctance to call fuch people *fuperftitious*; for, if they were fo, their fuperftition was of a moft amiable kind, and furely nothing fhort of the principles of this hellifh revolution could have hardened the hearts of men to fcourge them to death, and that merely becaufe they would not difgrace themfelves by receiving the facrament from the contaminated hands of an apoftate.

It were endlefs to enumerate all the dif-ferent forts of perfecution exercifed againft thofe who remained attached to their reli-gion. Little children were beaten half to death; the hair and ears of women were cut off; they were mounted on affes, and led about in the moft unfeemly and fhock-ing guife. The inftance of John Cantabel deferves particular notice. Cantabel was an honeft peafant, fincerely attached to the religion of his fathers. He happened to have a little catechifm which had been pub-liflhed by the non-juring clergy; it was found in his houfe; and this was a fufficient crime. A committee of municipal officers ordered the catechifm to be burnt; a great fire was made; Cantabel was brought forth, and commanded to throw the book into it. " No," fays the heroic peafant, it contains " the principles of my religion; it has been " my guide and my comfort, and it now " gives me the courage to tell you, that I " will never commit it to the flames." Upon this he was threatened, but ftill he remained refolute. One of the ruffians feized a flaming torch, and held it under his hand. " Burn on," faid he, " you " may burn not only my hand, but my " whole body, before I will do any thing " to difhonour my religion." He was afterwards mounted on a horfe, his back to the head, and the tail in his hand, and was thus conducted about amidft the fhouts of the rabble. The vile wretches, when tired with their fport, fuffered him to creep home, more dead than alive.—This is the *liberty of conscience* in the " *Age of Reason* !" This is the *toleration* we might expect from atheists, from thefe infidel philofophers, who are continually exclaiming againft the prejudices of their forefathers, and againft the fad effects of bigotry and religious zeal. In the cant of thefe *enlightened* reformers, this peafant was a *fanatic*, an *ariftocrat*, a *rebel to the law*, and, as fuch, they will tell you that he was worthy of death.

Notwithftanding the partial oppofition the apoftates met with, and the horror their conduct, as well as their miniftry excited in all good minds, they, at laft, found themfelves in poffeffion of the churches, to the exclufion of the ancient priefts. Such of thefe latter as had efcaped death, were now bereft of all means of fubfiftence; they were therefore obliged to become a charge to their faithful parifhioners. Had there been any fuch things as toleration and liberty under the Conftituent Affembly, thefe unfortunate men might ftill have found a retreat amongft their wealthy neighbours, that would have left them no reafon to regret the lofs of their falaries. But the greateft part of their wealthy neighbours were already reduced to their own fituation, and thofe who were not, knew that the reception of a non-juring prieft would amount to a proof of *ariftocracy*, fufficient to lead them to the guillotine. The expulfed prieſts were, then, obliged to take ſhelter in ſome obſcure and miſerable cabin, and often was the terror ſo great, that, like perſons infected with the plague, no one would admit them beneath his roof.

From ſuch a ſtate of miſery and humiliation ſome fled in diſguiſe to the countries ſurrounding France; ſome to receſſes in the foreſts, whither the peaſants of the neighbourhood brought them the means of exiſtence. Numbers, however, ſtill remained in their towns and villages. Seeing the whole country ſwarming with aſſaſſins, they thought, perhaps, they might as well wait the ſtab in their own pariſhes as to ſeek it at a diſtance. Many, too, from age and infirmity, were abſolutely incapable of travelling; and, beſides the ſmall remainder of a life ſo full of bitterneſs, could not, with ſuch men, be an object of ſufficient importance to induce them to abandon thoſe of their pariſhioners, who ſtill ſought their advice and conſolation. Some were retained by their affection to their relations, or their parents; it is ſo hard to break the bands of nature, to tear oneſelf from all one holds dear, that the riſk of death in competition with ſuch a ſeparation, loſes half its terrors.

The ancient prieſts who remained in their pariſhes, or near them, though often obliged to fecrete themfelves, and though, to appearances, generally fhunned, were reforted to by great numbers, particularly of the elderly people. I have already obferved, that, among the youth, there was a pretty general bias toward the apoftates. Hence enfued fuch fcenes of divifion and perfecution as no country on earth, except France, ever witneffed. Friends were divided againft friends; one branch of a family againft another. It often happened that the parents treated their children as apoftates, and the children their parents as ariftocrats; quarrels and bloodfhed were as often the confequences. We have feen (page 29 of *this volume*) a fon cut off the heads of his father and mother, becaufe they refufed to attend at the mafs of an apoftate, carry the heads to his club, and receive applaufes for the deed. Acts like this were not frequent; but others very near approaching it, were not only frequent but general. Sons, and even daughters, have been known to beat and lacerate their parents in the moft cruel manner. Hundreds of both fexes have been led to prifon and publicly accufed by their children. A man at Faulconberg in Artois, blew his wife's brains out with his mufket, and left her wallowing in her blood on the hearth with feven fmall children crying round her!

Can any man, with the common feelings
of humanity about his heart, contemplate
uch fcenes of horror, without execrating
:he revolution that gave rife to them ? *
The apoftate prielts failed not to fan the
flames of difcord and divifion. To ingratiate themfelves with the young and igno-
rant, they mixed in all their amufements
and debauches, treated them at their own
houfes, and inftituted civic feftivals for the
mob, with whom they were continually
furrounded. Their maffes were fung midft
the fhouts of robbers and murderers, and

* Many writers (and among others Thomas Paine)
have remarked, that the French paid great refpect,
even a fort of adoration, to old people : if this was the
cafe, which I am by no means inclined to deny, or
doubt, what fort of a revolution muft that be, which
has changed this refpect and veneration, fo juftly due
to old age, into fcorn and contempt, into a mercilefs
brutality, nay, into parricide ? *Solon* made no law to
punifh *facrilege* or *parricide* ; becaufe, he obferved,
" the firft was as yet unknown in Athens, and the
" fecond was fo directly againft all the feelings of na-
" ture, that he did not believe it could ever be com-
" mitted."—Poor *Solon* did not live in the " en=
" lightened eighteenth century," or he would never have
talked in this way. If he could but rife from the
grave, and liften to our *philofophers*, they would not
only convince him that fuch actions are poffible, but
they would tell him they were indifpenfably neceffary
to the eftablifhment of a free republican government.
Had *Solon* been at Paris, fince the revolution, he would
have been guillotined for a rank ariftocrat.

often interrupted by the arrival of fome innocent confcientious perfon, dragged in to
affift at what he looked upon as a profanation. Their churches refembled guard-
houfes, rather than places of divine worfhip. In proportion as they perceived themfelves negieĉted and defpifed, their wrath
againft their unfhaken predeceffors increafed. Vexed and humiliated to find, that all
the refpeĉtable part of their parifhioners
took as much pains to avoid them, as to
feek a communication with their old paftors, the whole weight of their vengeance
fell on thefe latter. In their exiftence itfelf
th-y faw a momento of their own infamy.
There is not a fpecies of cruelty, that the
moft obdurate can devife, which they left
uneffayed. They hunted them from their
retreats, from the houfes of their friends
and relations, from the woods and caverns
even, to expofe them to infult and murder.
The infirmities of age, the tears of parents,
nothing could foften the hearts of thefe
apoftate wretches. We have feen enough
of the fufferings of the old clergy in the
firft Chapter of this work; but there is yet
one inftance which I muft quote. " I was at
" *Trois Rivières* (fays *levoyageur de la Revo-*
" *lution*) a little village in Picardy. I faw
" feveral women running by the inn where
" I had put up; they all feemed much

" alarmed. I afked the landlord what was
" the matter: he told me that the revolu-
" tionary prieft, provoked to find that none
" of the village attended at his mafs, had
" been that morning to *Ville D'Eu* for a
" party of national guards, to aid him in
" driving the former prieft from a little
" cottage, where he and his mother had
" taken fhelter. The man gave me a moft
" affecting account of this good prieft, who
" was upwards of fourfcore years of age;
" and who had been the rector of that place
" for more than fifty years. On the day
" he was to deliver his cure into the hands
" of the apoftate, he fummoned his little
" flock to meet him in the church for the
" laft time. Not a foul was abfent: old or
" young. The women carried their infants
" in their arms, and two old people, not
" able to walk, were carried on couches. *My*
" *children*, fays the old man, *I have pref-*
" *fed your tender hands on the baptifmal*
" *font: I have fung the requiem for the fouls*
" *of your fathers: I muft now bid you an eter-*
" *nal farewel, deprived of the confolation of*
" *leaving my afhes amongft you.*"—Here he
" ceafed; tears ftifled his voice; the fobs
" and cries of his audience rendered the
" fcene too much for him. While the land-
" lord was fpeaking, we heard a difcharge
" of mufkets, and a loud fhriek of women.

T

"We ran to the spot. The peasants of the
"village, about forty in number, had af-
"sembled round the cottage with clubs to
"defend their pastor; but, the enemy hav-
"ing fire arms, they had been obliged to
"give way, leaving two of their compa-
"nions dead, and several wounded. I now
"held a sight sufficient to melt the heart
"of a tyger. Two ruffians of the national
"guard were dragging out this venerable
"old man by the hair of his head, by
"those locks as white as snow. He had
"received a wound in his cheek, from
"which the blood ran down on his gar-
"ments. In this situation was he led off,
"bare headed and bare footed, towards
"*Ville D'Eu,* while his poor old parent, who
"had been many years blind and dumb,
"remained on her bed, happily insensible
"of the sorrows of her son. As the villains
"pulled him along, all the words he was
"heard to utter, were, My Mother! Oh!
"My Mother!—The women and children
"of the village followed the escort with
"cries and lamentations, till the savages
"drove them back with the points of their
"bayonets."

Nor were those of the laity spared, who
resorted to the old clergy for the ex-
ercise of the rites which they looked upon
as essential. A new married couple having refused to have the ceremony performed

by one of the apoftates, a party of his myrmidons broke in among them the wedding night. The hufband made his efcape : the wife, in a fwoon, became the prey of the party. They gratified their brutal paffion, without gratifying their ferocity. They tore off her breafts, as a tyger might have done with his claws, and threw them on the floor. They then left her to wait till death relieved her from her horrible fituation *.

I fhould have fcrupled inferting a fact like this, though taken from fo refpectable a work, if the former part of this volume did not contain others, if poffible, furpaffing it : I fay, if *poffible*; for I declare I know not which is moft fhocking, the tearing off a woman's breafts, or the ripping a child from her womb, and fticking it on the point of a bayonet. Indeed, the greateft part of the facts related here, are fo much more fhocking and terrific than any thing

* *See Hift. of the French Clergy, page* 138.—I cannot help remarking here, that it is fomething wonderful this *Hiftory* is not more known in America.—It is a proof, among hundreds, how locked up we have been to every thing that might lead us to a juft eftimation of the French Revolution.—It is true, the greateft part of the News-papers have fet their faces againft truth ; but furely, were the preffes free, we ought not to fuffer ourfelves to be kept in the dark by people, who are, probably, paid for fo doing.

we have ever before had an idea of, that common murders appear as trifling.

By means like thefe, the old clergy and their adherents were extirpated, and religion along with them. The bufinefs of the new clergy (if the wretches deferve the name) was not to eftablifh one church on the ruins of another: it would be as prepofterous as to fuppofe that an Affembly of Atheifts and Deifts had any fuch intention, as to fuppofe that a horde of apoftates were calculated for the work. Thefe latter were, in fact, fo many miffionaries of blafphemy and murder, fent into the provinces purpofely to deftroy the ancient priefthood. The affembly forefaw that, when that was done, their new priefts would at any time become the apoftles of infidelity.

It muft be confidered that thefe legiflators did not want for cunning: an elegant writer has lately called them " architects of ruin;" and, indeed, they poffeffed the art of deftroying in its utmoft perfection. Their calculations with refpect to their new priefts were extremely juft; they came out to an unit. When they had annihilated their predeceffors, they were not only ready to fecond the decrees for the abolition of chriftianity altogether; they were not only inftrumental therein, but they had led the way. Several began to teach the religion of *Reason* in the Jacobin clubs, of which they were all members, and even in the pulpit. The garb of a prieft itfelf became a burthen to them, and they humbly afked leave to quit it for the more honourable one of the national guard. The apoftate bifhop of Moulin, who had been confecrated by the unhallowed hands of *Taillerand*, wrote to the Convention that he officiated with a pike and liberty cap, inftead of the crofier and the mitre. It was this vile wretch who firft caufed to be written on the gate of the burying-ground : " *this is the place of ever-* " *lafting fleep.*——

Three weeks after this communication of the bifhop of Moulin, *Gobet*, the new bifhop of Paris, with his Grand Vicars and three other revolutionary bifhops, came to the hall of the legiflators, and there abdicated chriftianity in form. They begged pardon of the injured nation for having fo long kept them in the dark, by duping them into a belief of the divinity of an *Impoftor*, whofe religion they now threw off with abhorrence, refolved in future to acknowledge no other deity than *Reafon* alone !

It was not more than four days after this that a pagan feftival was held in the Cathedral Church of Paris. A woman named Memoro, the wife of another man, but the ftrumpet of the vile Hebert, *alias* Father du Chêne, was dreffed up as the *goddefs of Reafon*. Her throne was of green turf; an altar was erected at fome diftance, on which the priefts burnt incenfe, while the legiflators and the brutified Parifian herd were proftrated before the throne of the goddefs *Reafon, alias* Memoro, *alias* du Chêne.

About this epoch appeared the paganifh republican calendar, with a decree ordering its adoption. This was intended to root from the poor tyranized people the very memory of religion; to dry up the only fource of comfort they had left. They had been robbed of all they poffeffed in this world, and their inexorable tyrants wifhed to rob them of every hope in the next. Some fay that this calendar itfelf was compofed by an apoftate prieft, others, that it was the work of a writer of farces, named Des Moulins. Whoever may be author, we know who has the honour of re-printing it and retailing it in this country.

It is true the laft mentioned acts, the confummation of the moft horrid blafphemy that ever man was witnefs of, took place under the Convention; but, what were they more than a neceffary confequence of the meafures of the Conftituent Affembly? nay, the leaders in that Affembly boafted, when they had obtained the decree againſt the non-juring prieſts, that they had tricked the people out of their religion, before they perceived it. Nor is there at this time one of thoſe who voted for that decree, who will not tell you, that chriſtianity is a farce, fit only for the amuſement of old folks, and that he rejoices in its abolition in France. This is not mere ſurmiſe.

Indeed, that their ſucceſſors have only fulfilled their wiſhes, in this reſpect, there can be no doubt, if any judgment of the wiſhes of men is to be formed from their principles, their words, and their actions. Who, I aſk, that wiſhed to preſerve religion, would have paſſed a decree for the expulſion of every prieſt that refuſed to forſwear himſelf? who, that did not wiſh to deſtroy religion, would have paſſed a decree for committing it to the care of apoſtates? Was it not clear, that ſuch men would ſtick at nothing? That, at the nod of their maſters, they would at any time be ready to blaſpheme the God they pretended to adore? On the contrary, the Aſſembly knew, that there was no hope of their ſyſtem taking root, while the ancient clergy remained in their cures. Among men, who gave up their all, and expoſed themſelves to almoſt certain death, rather than falſify their faith, they could not hope to find a *Gobet.* They could not hope to find fupple villains that would voluntarily depofe the emblems of their religion on the altar of a ftrumpet, and confefs themfelves to have been the crafty minifters of an *arch impoftor.*—

The oath tendered to the clergy was the touch-ftone; it was to prove them; to know whom the Affembly could depend on for the accomplifhment of their projects, and whom they could not depend on. The enforcing of the oath was the laft blow to public religion in France, and therefore the deftruction of that religion, with all its immoral and murderous confequences, is due to the Conftituent Affembly, and to them alone. It is as nonfenfical as unjuft to accufe this or that faction, or even the Convention itfelf, of exchanging Chriftianity for a fyftem of paganifm; infidels who adore an idol are as good as infidels who adore none; and where is the difference, whether the adored idol be Jean Jacques Rouffeau or Madame Memoro? An adultrefs is as good a goddefs as an adulterer is a god at any time.

Let the reader now look back, and he will eafily trace all the horrors of the French Revolution to the decrees of the Conftituent Affembly. It was they that rent the government to pieces; it was they that firft broached the deftructive doctrine of equality; it was they that deftroyed all ideas of private property; and finally, it was they that rendered the people hardened, by effacing from their minds every principle of the only religion capable of keeping mankind within the bounds of juftice and humanity. Look alfo at their particular actions, and you will fee them breaking their oaths to their conftituents and to their king; you will fee their agents driving people from their eftates, beating and killing them; you will fee them furrounded with a fet of hireling writers and affaffins, employed to degrade and murder peaceable people attached to the religion of their forefathers; and you will fee them not only pardoning murderers, in fpite of their poor humiliated monarch, but even receiving the affaffins at their bar, covering them with applaufes, and inflituting feftivals in their honour. What have the members of the Convention and their agents done more than this? They have murdered in greater numbers. True; but what have numbers to do with the matter? The principle on which thofe murders was committed was ever the fame; it was more or lefs active as occafion required. The wants of the Convention were more preffing than thofe of the Conftituent Affembly. The Affembly were not driven to the expedient of *requifitions,* nor was the hour yet arrived for the promulgation of the paganiſh calendar. Conſequently they met with leſs oppoſition, and therefore leſs murders were neceſſary; but, had they continued their ſittings to this day, the devaſtation of every kind would have been the ſame that it has been.

The whole hiſtory of the revolution preſents us with nothing but a regular progreſs in robbery and murder. The firſt Aſſembly, for inſtance, begin by flattering the mob, wheedling their king out of his title and his power; they then ſet him at defiance, proſcribe or put to death his friends; and then ſhut him up in his palace, as a wild beaſt in a cage. The ſecond Aſſembly ſend a gang of ruffians to inſult and revile him, and then they hurl him from his throne. The third Aſſembly cut his throat. What is there in all this but a regular and natural progreſſion from bad to worſe. And ſo with the reſt of their abominable actions.

To throw the blame on the ſucceſſors of the firſt deſpotic Aſſembly is ſuch a perverſion of reaſon, ſuch an abandonment of truth, that no man, who has a ſingle grain of ſenſe, can hear of with patience. As well might we aſcribe all the murders committed at Nantz to the under cut-throats, by whom they were perpetrated, and not to the Convention by whoſe order, and un-

der whofe protection, thefe cut-throats
acted. The Conftituent Affembly knew
the confequences of their decrees, as well as
Foucault (*See page* 66.) knew the confequence of his order for throwing forty women from the cliff Pierre-moine into the fea ;
and it is full as ridiculous to hear them pretend, that they did not wifh thofe confequences to follow, as it would be to ear Foucault pretend, that he did not wifh the forty
women fhould be drowned. True, the
Convention are guilty of every crime under
heaven : affaffins and blafphemers muft ever
merit deteftation and abhorrence, from whatever motive they may act, or by whomfoever
taught and inftigated ; but ftill the pre-emi-
nence in infamy is due to their teachers and
inftigators : the Convention is, in relation to
the Conftituent Affembly, what the igno-
rant defperate bravo is in relation to his
crafty and fculking employer.

Before I conclude, it may not be improper, as I have hitherto fpoken of the Conftituent Affembly in a general way, to
make fome diftinctions with refpect to the
perfons who compofed it. I am very far
from holding them all up as objects of abhorrence, or even of cenfure. There were
many, very many, men of great wifdom
and virtue, who were elected to the States-
General, and even who joined the Affem-

bly, after it affumed the epithet *National.*
It would be the height of injuftice to reproach thefe men with the confequences of
meafures, which they oppofed with fuch
uncommon eloquence and courage. Hiftory will make honourable mention of their
names, when the epitome I have here attempted will be loft and forgotten. Suffice
it then to fay, that the weight of our cenfure, of the cenfure of all juft and good
men, ought to fall on thofe licentious poli-
ticians and infidel philofophers alone, who
fanctioned the decree for the annihilation of
property and religion.

Here, too, we ought to diveft ourfelves
of every thing of a perfonal or party nature, and direct our abhorrence to principles alone. As to the actors, they have,
in general, already expiated their wicked-
nefs or folly by the lofs of their lives. We
have feen the atheift Condorcet obliged to
fly in difguife from the capital, the inhabitants of which he had corrupted, and by
whom he had been adored as the great lu-
minary of the age : we have feen him af-
fume the garb and the fupplicating tone of
a common beggar, lurking in the lanes and
woods, like a houfelefs thief, and, at laft,
literally dying in a ditch, leaving his carcafe a prey to the fowls of the air, and his
memory as a leffon to future apoftles of

anarchy and blafphemy. Scores, not to fay hundreds, of his coadjutors have fhared a fate little different from his own ; and thofe who have not, can have little reafon to congratu-late themfelves on their efcape. The tornado they have raifed for the deftruction of others, has fwept them from the feat of their tyran-ny, and fcattered them over every corner of the earth. Thofe haughty ufurpers, who refufed the precedence to the fucceffors of Charlemagne, are now obliged to yield it to a peafant or a porter. They who de-creed, that the " Folding-Doors of the Louvre fhould fly open at their approach," are now glad to lift the latch of a wicket, and bend their heads beneath the thatch of a cabin. And, what language can exprefs the vexation, the anguifh, the cutting re-flections, that muft be the companions of their obfcurity ! When they look back on their diftracted country, when they behold the widows, the orphans, the thoufands and hundreds of thoufands of murdered victims, that it prefents ; when they behold the frantic people, carrying the dagger to the hearts of their parents, nay, digging their forefathers from their graves, and throwing their afhes to the winds ; when they behold all this, and reflect that it is the work of their own hands, well might

U

they call on the hills to hide them. The torments of fuch an exiftence who can bear? Next to the wrath of heaven, the malediction of one's country is furely the molt tremendous and infupportable.

***

Now, what is the advantage we ought to derive from the awful example before us?—It ought to produce in us a watchfulnefs, and a fteady refolution to oppoſe the advances of diforganizing and infidel principles. I am aware that it will be faid by fome, that all fear of the progrefs of thefe principles is imaginary; but, conftant obfervation affures me, that it is but too well founded. Let any man examine the change in political and religious opinions fince the eſtablifhment of the general government, and particularly the change crept in along with our filly admiration of the French Revolution, and fee if the refult of his inquiries does not juftify a fear of our falling under the fcourge that has brought a happy and gallant people on their knees, and left them bleeding at every pore.

Unfortunately for America, Great Britain has thrown from her the principles of the French revolutionifts with indignation and abhorrence. This, which one would

imagine fhould have had little or no influence on us, has ferved, in fome meafure, as a
guide to our opinions, and has been one of
the principal motives for our actions. A combination of circumftances, fuch as, perhaps,
never before met together, has fo foured
the minds of the great mafs of the people
in this country, has worked up their hatred
againft Great Britain to fuch a pitch, that
the inftant that nation is named, they lofe
not only their temper but their reafon alfo.
The dictates of nature and the exercife of
judgment are thrown afide : whatever the
Britifh adopt muft be rejected, and whatever they reject muft be adopted. Hence it
is, that all the execrable acts of the French
legiflators, not forgetting their murders and
their blafphemy, have met with the moft
unqualified applaufes, merely becaufe they
were execrated in the ifland of Britain.

The word *Republic* has alfo done a great
deal. France is a *Republic*, and the decrees of the legiflators were neceffary to
maintain it a Republic. This *word* out-
weighs, in the eftimation of fome perfons,
(I wifh I could fay they are few in number)
all the horrors that have been, and that
can be, committed in that country. One of
thefe modern republicans will tell you that
he does not deny, that hundreds of thoufands of innocent perfons have been mur-

U 2

dered in France; that the people have neither religion nor morals; that all the ties of
nature are rent afunder; that the rifing
generation will be a race of cut-throats;
that poverty and famine ftalk forth at large;
that the nation is half depopulated; that its
riches along with millions of the beft of the
people are gone to enrich and aggrandize its
enemies; that its commerce, its manufac-
tures, its fciences, its arts, and its honour,
are no more; but at the end of all this, he
will tell you that it muft be happy, becaufe
it is a *Republic*. I have heard more than one
of thefe republican zealots declare, that he
would fooner fee the laft of the French ex-
tirminated, than fee them adopt any other
form of government. Such a fentiment is
characteriftic of a mind locked up in favage
ignorance; and I would no more truft my
throat within the reach of fuch a republican,
than I would within that of a Louvet a
Gregoire, or any of their colleagues.

Our enlightened philofophers run on in
a fine canting ftrain about the bigotry and
ignorance of their anceftors; but, I would
afk them, what more ftupid doltifh bigotry
can there be, than to make the found of a
word the ftandard of good or bad government? what is there in the combination of
the letters which make up the word *Republic*; what is there in the found they pro-

duce, that the bellowing of it forth fhould compenfate for the want of every virtue, and even for common fenfe and common honefty ? It is fynonymous with liberty.—Fatal error! In the mouth of a turbulent demagogue it is fynonymous with liberty, and with every thing elfe, that will pleafe its hearers; but, with the man of virtue and fenfe, it has no more than its literal value; that is, it means, of itfelf, neither good nor evil. If we call our own government that of a *Republic*, and judge of the meaning of the word by the effects of that government, it will admit of a moft amiable interpretation; but, if we are to judge of it by what it has produced in France, it means all that is ruinous, tyrannical, blafphemous and bloody. Laft winter, one of thefe republican heroes in Congrefs, accufed a gentleman from New England of having adopted *anti-republican* principles, becaufe he propofed fomething that feemed to militate *againft negro-flavery!* Thus, then, republicanifm did not mean liberty. In fhort, it means any thing: it is a watch word of faction, and if ever our happy and excellently conftituted Republic fhould be overturned, it will be done under the mafk of republicanifm.

Let us, then, be upon our guard; let us look to the characters and actions of men, and not to their profeffions; let us attach ourfelves to things and not to words; to fenfe and not to found. Should the day of *requifition* and *murder* arrive, our tyrants calling themfelves republicans will be but a poor confolation to us. The lofs of property, the preffure of want, beggary, will not be lefs real becaufe flowing from republican decrees. Hunger pinches the republican, the cold blaft cramps his joints as well as thofe of other men. This word does not foften the pangs of death. The keen knife will not produce a delectable fenfation becaufe drawn acrofs the throat by a republican; nor will the word republican parry a bullet, or render a flaming fire a bed of down. When Monfieur Berthier had the ghaftly head of his father preffed againft his lips, when his own heart was afterwards torn from his living body, and placed, all reeking and palpitating, on a table before a committee of magiftrates, the agonies of his mind and of his mangled carcafs were not affuaged by the fhouts of his republican murderers.

Shall we fay that thefe things never can take place among us? Becaufe we have hitherto preferved the character of a pacific and humane people, fhall we fet danger at defiance? Though we are not French-

·men, we are men as well as they, and con-
fequently are liable to be mifled, and even
to be funk to the loweft degree of brutality as they have been. They, too, had an
amiable character : what character have
they now ? The fame principles brought
into action among us would produce the
fame degradation. I repeat we are not
what we were before the French Revolution. Political projectors from every corner
of Europe, troublers of fociety of every defcription, from the whining philofophical
hypocrite to the daring rebel and more daring blafphemer, have taken fhelter in thefe
States. Will it be pretended that the principles and paffions of thefe men have changed with the change of air ? it would be folly
to fuppofe it.

Nor are men of the fame ftamp wanting
among the native Americans. There is not
a fingle action of the French revolutionifts,
but has been juftified and applauded in our
public papers, and meny of them in our
public affemblies. Anarchy has its open
advocates. The divine author of our religion has been put upon a level with the in-.
famous Marat. We have feen a clergyman·
of the epifcopal church publicly abufed, becaufe he had recommended to his congregation to bewa.e of the atheiftical principles

of the French. Even their calendar, the frivolous offspring of infidelity, is proposed for our imitation. Where perfons, whofe livelihood depends on their daily publication, are to be found who are ever ready to publifh articles of this nature, it were the groffeft folly not to believe, that there are hundreds and thoufands to whom they give pleafure. * But, we are not left to mere furmife here. How many numerous companies have iffued, under the form of toafts, fentiments offenfive to humanity, and difgraceful to our national character? We have feen the *guillotine* toafted to three times three cheers, and even under the difcharge of cannon. If drunken men, as is ufually the cafe, fpeak from the bottom of their hearts, what quarter fhould we have to expect from wretches like thefe. It muft be allowed, too, that where the cannons were fired to give eclat to fuch a fen-

---

* It is a truth that no one will deny, that the News-papers of this country have become its fcourge. I fpeak with a few exceptions. It is faid that they enlighten the people; but their light is like the torch of an incendiary, and the one has the fame deftructive effect on mind as the other has on matter. The whole ftudy of the editors feems to be to deceive and confound. One would almoft think they were hired by fome malicious demon, to turns the brains and corrupt the hearts of their readers.

·timent, that the convives were not of the
.moft defpicable clafs. And, what would
the reader fay, were I to tell him of a mem-
.ber of Congrefs, who wifhed to fee one of
·thofe murderous machines, employed for
lopping off the heads of the French, permanent in the State-Houfe yard of the City of
Philadelphia ?

If thefe men of blood had fucceeded in
plunging us into a war : if they had once
got the fword into their hands, they would
have mowed us down like ftubble. The
word *ariftocrat* would have been employed
to as good account here, as ever it has been
in France. We might 'ere this, have feen
-our places of worfhip turned into ftables;
-we might have feen the banks of the Delaware, like thofe of the Loire, covered with
human carcafes, and its waters tinged with
blood : 'ere this we might have feen our
parents butchered, and even the head of
our admired and beloved Prefident rolling
on a fcaffold.

I know the reader will ftart back with
horror. His heart will tell him, that it is
impoffible. But, once more, let him look
at the example before us. The man who,
in 1788, fhould have predicted the fate of
the laft humane and truly patriotic Louis,
would have been treated as a wretch or a

· madman. The attacks on the character and conduct of the irreproachable *Washington*, have been as bold, if not bolder, than those which led to the downfal of the unfortunate French Monarch. His impudent and unprincipled enemies have reprefented him as cankered with every vice that mark a worthlefs tyrant ; they have callled him the betrayer of the liberties of his country, and have even drawn up and publifhed *articles of accufation* againft him ! 'Can it, then, be imagined, that, had they poffeffed the power, they wanted the will to dip their hands in his blood ? I am fully affured, that thefe wretches do not make a hundred thoufandth part of the people of the Union : the name of *Washington* is as dear and dearer, to all good men, than it ever was. But, of what confequence is their affection to him, of what avail to themfelves, if they fuffer him to be thus treated, without making one fingle effort to defeat the project of his infamous traducers ? It is not for me to dictate the method of doing this ; but fure I am, that had the friends of virtue and order fhown only a hundredth part of the zeal in the caufe of their own country, as the enemies of both have done in the caufe of France, we fhould not now have to lament the exiftence of a hardened and

(239)

mpious faction, whofe deftructive princi-
)les, if not timely and firmly oppofed,
nay one day render the annals of America
is difgraceful as thofe of the French Re-
/olution.

T H E   E N D.

www.ingramcontent.com/pod-product-compliance
Lightning Source LLC
Chambersburg PA
CBHW030407270326
41926CB00009B/1309